REDEMPTION

THE **BALTIMORE RAVENS'** 2012 CHAMPIONSHIP SEASON

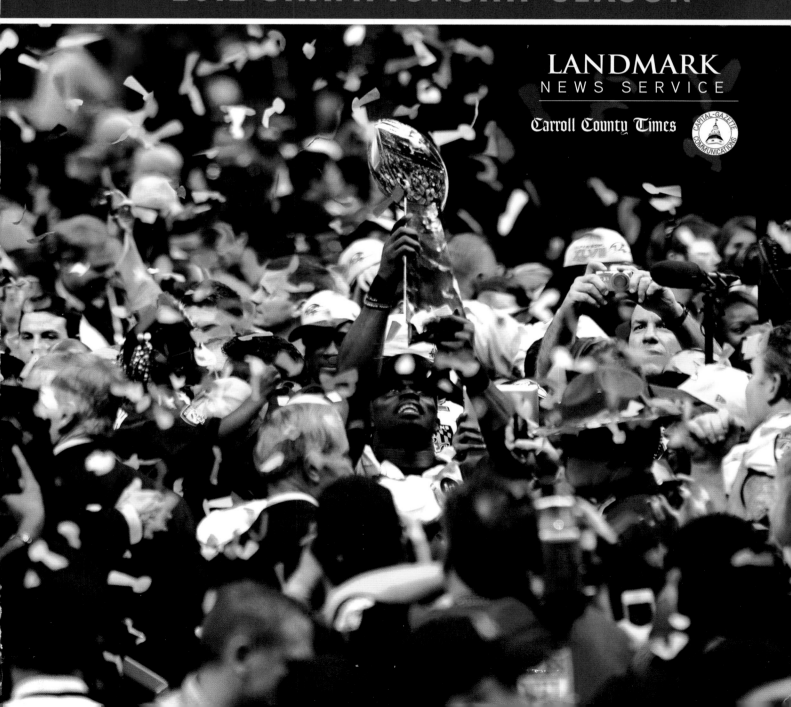

LANDMARK
NEWS SERVICE

Carroll County Times

CAPITAL-GAZETTE COMMUNICATIONS

Ravens head coach John Harbaugh holds the Lombardi Trophy following the Ravens' win over the San Francisco 49ers in Super Bowl XLVII. The 49ers are coached by Jim Harbaugh, John's brother. AP Images

This book is book is available in quantity at special discounts for your group or organization.
For further information, contact:

Triumph Books LLC
814 North Franklin Street
Chicago, Illinois 60610
Phone: (312) 337-0747
www.triumphbooks.com

Printed in U.S.A.
ISBN: 978-1-60078-883-3

Carroll County Times
Pat Richardson, Publisher
Jim Lee, Editor
Bob Blubaugh, Sports Editor
Matt Zenitz, Ravens beat writer
Dylan Slagle, Photographer
Rich Dubroff, Correspondent
Brian Haines, Copy Editor
Ken Koons, Photographer
Dave Munch, Photographer
Pat Stoetzer, Staff writer

Content packaged by Mojo Media, Inc.
Joe Funk: Editor
Jason Hinman: Creative Director

Front cover photo by Getty Images. Back cover photo by DYLAN SLAGLE/STAFF.

CONTENTS

Introduction

By Bob Blubaugh

The Baltimore Ravens' championship season did not begin on the NFL's opening weekend in September. Nor did it begin when training camp started in late July. Or even during organized team activities in the spring.

The Ravens' run to the Super Bowl XLVII title began on Jan. 22, 2012, in the visitor's locker room inside Gillette Stadium, home of the New England Patriots.

The Ravens' 2011 season had just ended in excruciating fashion, with Lee Evans unable to hang onto what would've been an AFC Championship game-winning touchdown pass and Billy Cundiff missing on a 32-yard field goal that would've sent the game to overtime.

Middle linebacker Ray Lewis, the emotional leader of the Ravens, told his teammates not to drop their heads; that the loss would make them stronger.

"We gotta come back and go to work to make sure we finish it next time," he said.

Improbably, that's exactly what they did. For the second time in franchise history, they are Super Bowl champions.

Despite major injuries that sidelined 2011 Defensive Player of the Year Terrell Suggs for half the season, top cornerback Lardarius Webb for the final 10 games and the playoffs and Lewis himself for 10 games. Despite tragedies that included the deaths of team patriarch Art Modell and the younger brother of wide receiver Torrey Smith. Despite the unusual move of firing offensive coordinator Cam Cameron in December. Despite losing four of their final five regular-season games. Despite being 70 yards away from a loss and elimination in the final minute of a road playoff game. And despite a power failure inside the Superdome that halted the Super Bowl and the Ravens' momentum.

They earned redemption for that heartbreaking loss in last season's AFC title game, first by avenging that defeat in New England with an AFC Championship celebration on the Patriots' field, and then by hoisting the Lombardi Trophy after a nerve-wracking 34-31 win in a bizarre Super Bowl XLVII.

"Look at what we have been through," running back Ray Rice said during the playoff run. "We've been through a lot of adversity this year. To overcome the things that we have overcome, to be counted out, to be not good enough at times … is definitely a humbling feeling."

The question, "Can Joe Flacco lead the Ravens to a Super Bowl title?" will never again be asked. The oft-criticized quarterback capped a remarkable postseason run, during which he threw 11 touchdown passes without an interception, by being named Super Bowl MVP. He completed 22 of 33 passes for 287 yards and three touchdowns.

"Joe is phenomenal," head coach John Harbaugh said afterward.

Flacco's strong right arm staked the Ravens to a 28-6 lead early in the third quarter and he

remained his normal, unflappable self when the game got close.

"He was laughing and having fun. He was poised, relaxed and confident," tight end Dennis Pitta said. "That's why he is a great player. He doesn't change in tough situations."

This Super Bowl was quite a tough situation.

It figured to be remembered for pitting John Harbaugh against his brother, Jim, as well as for being the final game in Lewis' certain Hall of Fame career.

It will also be remembered as the Super Bowl delayed for more than 30 minutes by a power failure. The 49ers used the stoppage to their advantage, rallying to make it close, but never catching the Ravens.

Lewis and the rest of the defense stood tall on four goal-to-go plays in the final minutes, securing a win and finishing off a remarkable season that much more than made up for the disappointment of 2011.

"It was an up-and-down rollercoaster," Lewis said, after capping his "last ride" with his second Super Bowl title.

Indeed, there was the 5-1 start. The catastrophic injuries. The three-game losing streak in December. The replacing of Cameron with Jim Caldwell. The miraculous, overtime playoff win in Denver. The revenge earned in New England. And, finally, the celebration in the Superdome as confetti fell.

Harbaugh, whose five seasons with the Ravens have produced five playoff appearances and now a first Super Bowl title for owner Steve Bisciotti and longtime standout players like Ed Reed, Terrell Suggs and Haloti Ngata, summed it up best.

"We are a very resilient team," he said. "All the guys that worked so hard, stuck together through trials, tribulations, difficulties and maintained faith. It feels like they got what they deserve."

They got redemption, and more. ∎

Veteran safety Ed Reed hoists the Lombardi Trophy following Baltimore's triumph in New Orleans.
DYLAN SLAGLE/STAFF PHOTO

SUPER BOWL XLVII • FEBRUARY 3, 2013
New Orleans, Louisiana • Ravens 34, 49ers 31

Lights Out

Ravens overcome adversity to win Super Bowl
By Matt Zenitz

It was fitting that a season filled with so many obstacles would be decided by the Baltimore Ravens' ability to overcome one final bit of adversity.

Despite a power outage early in the second half that swung the momentum of a game during which the Ravens appeared to be pulling away — and despite a San Francisco 49ers scoring run that put them in position for a game-winning touchdown in the closing minutes — the Ravens end the 2012 season, and end linebacker Ray Lewis' "last ride," as Super Bowl XLVII champions, holding on to defeat the 49ers 34-31 behind MVP Joe Flacco to claim the second Super Bowl title in franchise history.

Baltimore led 28-6 early in the third quarter before a power outage at the Mercedes-Benz Superdome that suspended play for 32 minutes. What followed the delay was a 23-6 scoring run by the 49ers that put San Francisco in a position — trailing by five points with just more than four minutes remaining in the fourth quarter — to drive for a potentially game-deciding touchdown in the game's closing minutes.

The 49ers drove to Baltimore's 5-yard line, but Colin Kaepernick's fourth-down pass attempt fell incomplete and, despite everything that transpired during the second half — and despite everything that transpired throughout the course of the season — the Ravens were Super Bowl champions.

"It's never pretty," Baltimore coach John Harbaugh said after beating his brother, 49ers coach Jim Harbaugh. "It's never perfect. But it's us. ... This feels great!"

Ravens tight end Dennis Pitta said he felt the game turning.

"Oh my goodness. I mean, we had a ton of momentum ... then the power goes out and we're waiting for what felt like an hour. We lost a lot of momentum and, credit goes to [the 49ers], they came storming back," he said. "But this team has continued to fight and never quit. What a fitting [end]. ... It didn't make it easy, but it was fun."

Baltimore led 21-6 at halftime, and it extended its lead even more when Jacoby Jones returned the opening kickoff of the second half of 108 yards for a touchdown. But after defensive end Art Jones sacked Kaepernick to force a third-and-13 on the 49ers' ensuing possession, the power went

Anquan Boldin makes a catch in front of 49ers cornerback Carlos Rogers in the second half. Boldin caught six passes for 104 yards. DYLAN SLAGLE/STAFF PHOTO

Ravens kicker Justin Tucker carries the football on a fake field goal attempt during the second quarter. The play — the first fake field goal attempt in Super Bowl history — came up one yard short of a first down. DYLAN SLAGLE/STAFF PHOTO

out in the Superdome. And in a bizarre scene, the Ravens and 49ers were forced to wait on the sideline for more than 30 minutes as power was restored in the stadium.

When play resumed, a Baltimore offense that was on fire for much of the first half had gone flat while a San Francisco offense that was stagnant for much of the previous two-plus quarter all of a sudden came to life.

Kaepernick led scoring drives of the 49ers' next four possessions, trimming what was a 22-point deficit prior to the power outage to just 31-29 with just less than 10 minutes remaining in the fourth quarter.

And after the Ravens drove for a Justin Tucker field goal on their ensuing possession, Kaepernick and the 49ers took over at their 20-yard line trailing just 34-29 with a little more than four minutes remaining in the fourth quarter.

San Francisco worked the ball to Baltimore's 5-yard line. But facing a fourth-and-goal at the Ravens' 5, Kaepernick was pressured by Baltimore linebacker Dannell Ellerbe and his fourth-down pass attempt sailed beyond the reach of wide receiver Michael Crabtree.

The 49ers got one final shot with the ball — as the Ravens were forced to punt to Ted Ginn with four seconds left in the fourth quarter — but Ginn was brought down at midfield as time expired, and the Ravens were officially Super Bowl champions.

"It feels good," Harbaugh said. "It feels really good actually. I would like to be more profound than that, but I do not have those words. ... It feels like all the guys that worked so hard, stuck together through trials, tribulations, difficulties and maintained faith — it feels like they got what they deserve."

This is a team that dealt with the death of former owner Art Modell. It dealt with the death of wide receiver Torrey Smith's younger brother. It dealt with an exorbitant amount of injuries to key defensive players. It dealt with prolonged offensive struggles that resulted in the team firing offensive coordinator Cam Cameron with just four weeks remaining in the regular season. And it went through a three-game losing streak late in

San Francisco quarterback Colin Kaepernick works to elude Haloti Ngata and Ray Lewis during the first half. The young 49ers quarterback started slow, but led four consecutive scoring drives in the second half to close the Ravens' lead to 31-29 with less than 10 minutes remaining in the game. DYLAN SLAGLE/STAFF PHOTO

Defensive end Arthur Jones recovers a fumble by San Francisco's LaMichael James in the second quarter. Jones later sacked 49ers quarterback Colin Kaepernick in the third quarter, the last play before the lights went out at the Mercedes-Benz Superdome. DYLAN SLAGLE/STAFF PHOTO

the regular season that had many on a national level doubting the Ravens' viability as a Super Bowl contender heading into the playoffs.

But the team persevered, just as it did Sunday night.

"We're certainly glad it turned out the way it did," Baltimore offensive coordinator Jim Caldwell said. "[The power outage] was a slight interruption, but we've had a lot of adversity all through this season, and that was just another blip on the radar screen."

Added Harbaugh: "We have a lot of resolve. That's why we won the game."

Flacco was named MVP. The quarterback that's been so heavily scrutinized on both a local and a national level since entering the league in 2008 completed a career-defining postseason run with 287 yards and three touchdowns against a 49ers defense that ranked as the NFL's fourth-best against the pass during the regular season.

All three of his scoring passes came during the first half, including an electrifying 56-yard touchdown pass to Jones that pushed Baltimore's lead to 21-3 with just less than two minutes remaining in the second quarter.

Flacco was 13-of-19 for 192 yards with the three scoring passes during the first half.

He completed the postseason with 11 touchdown passes, tying a record for a single postseason, and without a single interception.

"I am a Joe Flacco fan," said Lewis, who was playing in the final game of his storied 17-year career. "I've been a Joe Flacco fan. For him to come in and do what he did today, and make some of the throws he made, that is what we've always seen. But we've always said that when you win a championship, one man won't win the ring. It will be a complete team. Today, we won as a complete team."

But it's a win that may not have culminated without that final defensive stop.

The 49ers finished with 468 yards of total offense, 289 of which came after the power outage. They got 302 yards through the air from Kaepernick and a combined 172 yards from Kaepernick and Frank Gore on the ground. But, in the game's biggest moment, and on the final defensive snap of Lewis' career, the Ravens defense came up with a stop, forcing the incomplete pass from

Running back Ray Rice carries the ball in the first half. The veteran back ran for 59 yards and caught four passes for 19 yards. DYLAN SLAGLE/ STAFF PHOTO

Kaepernick that resulted in a turnover on downs with one minute, 46 remaining in the fourth quarter.

"What a fitting way to end that game — our defense on the field and Ray Lewis in his last play," Pitta said. "They came up huge on the goal-line and got the stop."

It's a stop that propelled the Ravens to the Super Bowl title, and a stop that provides an exclamation point on the illustrious career of Lewis.

The future Hall-of-Famer announced his plans to retire at the end of the season in the week leading up to the Ravens' playoff opener against the Indianapolis Colts. Less than a month later, he ends his career as a world champion.

"What better way to go out? And, I think, more importantly, it was my teammates in the way I went out — the things we've been through all year," Lewis said. "[We were] tested through this journey, it was an up-and-down rollercoaster — the injuries, the people — and we stayed together. And now, I get to ride off into the sunset with my second ring." ■

Opposite: Ravens defensive backs Ed Reed and Jimmy Smith defend as Colin Kaepernick's fourth down pass sails wide of receiver Michael Crabtree in the final minutes of Super Bowl XLVII. Above: San Francisco cornerback Tarrell Brown breaks up a pass intended for Torrey Smith.
DYLAN SLAGLE/STAFF PHOTOS

Unflappable Flacco Named Super Bowl MVP

Quarterback proves he's amongst game's elite

By Pat Stoetzer

Joe Flacco came to Super Bowl XLVII with impressive postseason credentials — gaudy statistics like the most career road victories in history and eight touchdowns with no interceptions in this year's playoffs — all the while displaying the nothing-bothers-me demeanor that led to Baltimore fans dubbing him "Joe Cool."

The Ravens quarterback added another accolade Sunday night in New Orleans — Super Bowl MVP.

Flacco led Baltimore to a 34-31 win over San Francisco with another solid performance, using his powerful right arm as a statement toward his status in the NFL. He also used it to raise the Lombardi Trophy, to the delight of the thousands of Ravens fans inside the Superdome.

The 28-year-old threw for 287 yards and three touchdowns, connecting on 22 of 33 passes along the way. Baltimore held on to win despite a furious San Francisco rally led by second-year quarterback Colin Kaepernick (302 passing yards, 62 rushing yards), but the 49ers came up short on their final series near the goal line and the Ravens prevailed.

With Flacco at the top.

"I don't think it's going to settle in for a while," Flacco said. "We don't make anything easy."

Flacco finished the playoffs with 11 touchdowns, tying Joe Montana and Kurt Warner for the most in a postseason. He also became the sixth player in NFL history to throw three or more touchdowns in the first half of a Super Bowl. One of them was a 56-yard bomb to speedster Jacoby Jones in the second quarter.

Flacco also made a few other pivotal throws that helped Baltimore keep its lead, particularly midway through the fourth quarter in a huge third-down situation.

Baltimore faced a third-and-inches at its own 45 with 7 minutes, 14 seconds to play, and Flacco hit receiver Anquan Boldin, his main target during the Super Bowl, for 15 yards to keep the Ravens' offense on the field and the clock on the move.

"I told Joe to give me a chance," said Boldin, who caught six passes for 104 yards, "and he gave it to me."

Ravens coach John Harbaugh didn't hesitate to eschew a running play on third-and-short with Flacco under center.

"To me, it shows you he has got guts," Harbaugh said. "He has got the guts of a burglar. He was doing it all night, making plays."

Joe Flacco throws a 1-yard touchdown pass to tight end Dennis Pitta to give the Ravens a 14-3 lead midway through the second quarter. DYLAN SLAGLE/STAFF PHOTO

The drive didn't end with a touchdown, but Flacco moved the ball 60 yards and used 5:38 with three completions for 26 yards. Then he watched from the bench while the Ravens' defense kept Kaepernick and the Niners out of the end zone for the go-ahead score.

And perhaps Flacco proved some of his naysayers wrong with his Super Bowl performance.

"I've never cared," Flacco said. "I don't ever want to feel like I'm in a position to defend myself, it's just not right. We'll have this thing forever. Everybody on that team will be connected to each other forever and that's something pretty special."

He threw for a career high 3,817 yards in the regular season and tossed 22 touchdowns with 10 interceptions, but Flacco and the offense went through enough struggles that coach John Harbaugh switched coordinators during the year, firing Cam Cameron and replacing him with Jim Caldwell. In the new offensive coordinator's second game, Flacco led the Ravens to a 33-14 win over the Giants on Dec. 23 with 309 yards on 25-for-36 passing and two touchdowns.

Flacco threw for 1,140 yards in the playoffs and completed 57.9 percent of his passes in beating Indianapolis, Denver, New England, and San Francisco.

The Ravens will attempt to negotiate a long-term contract with Flacco during the offseason. Flacco was in the final year of his rookie contract. A championship and Super Bowl MVP will only help Flacco's leverage.

"It's tough to put into words because it really hasn't sunk in yet," Flacco said. "I don't even think it has sunk in yet that we're here. Pretty cool." ∎

Super Bowl MVP Joe Flacco holds up the Vince Lombardi Trophy following the Ravens' upset of the favored San Francisco 49ers. Flacco completed 22 of 33 passes for 287 yards and three touchdowns. DYLAN SLAGLE/STAFF PHOTO

Ravens Patriarch Modell Dies At 87

Influential owner moved franchise to Baltimore

By Matt Zenitz • September 6, 2012

Baltimore Ravens patriarch Art Modell, as beloved in Baltimore as he was reviled in Cleveland, died early early Thursday at age 87. Modell moved the Browns to Baltimore in 1996, returning football to a city that had been without since the Colts moved to Indianapolis in 1984. He was the Ravens' majority owner through the 2003 season.

"When you think about Art Modell, you think about a great man, a leader, a father and a servant," said Ray Lewis, the Ravens' standout middle linebacker since 1996, in a statement. "I genuinely loved Art as a man, and he showed me what to strive for in life. When you truly see the impact he had on everyone he touched, it humbles you.

"When I found out he wasn't doing well, I knew immediately I had to see him. When I was with him [Wednesday], I prayed with him and shared with him things that a son would say to a father. Even though he has left us, he is going to a place that one day we all want to be. I am truly blessed to have had Art in my life. He was a humble servant, and one of the best men I have ever known."

Modell was surrounded by family when he died.

"Sadly, I can confirm that my father died peacefully of natural causes at 4 this morning," David Modell said in a statement. "My brother, John Modell, and I were with him when we finally rejoined the absolute love of his life, my mother Pat Modell, who passed away last October.

"He was adored by the entire Baltimore community for his kindness and generosity. And, he loved Baltimore. He made an important and indelible contribution to the lives of his children, grandchildren and his entire community. We will miss him."

Modell was one of the most influential figures in NFL history.

He was a team owner for 43 years, served as NFL president (1967-69), the only elected president in league history, was chairman of the Owners Labor Committee, which successfully negotiated the NFL's first players' collective bargaining agreement, and served on the NFL-AFL Merger Committee, breaking the impasse for realignment of the two leagues by moving the Browns to the AFC.

"I've had a love affair with this league for 40 years. I've watched it grow and grow and grow into something extraordinary," Modell told the *Carroll County Times* in 2003. "I'm proud of my career.... It was a great run."

Modell was chairman of the NFL's Television Committee for 31 years (1962-93), worked closely with former NFL commissioner Pete Rozelle to establish NFL Films, and later became the first chairman of NFL Films, and was an important negotiator with ABC to start *Monday Night Football*.

"I believe very strongly that Art Modell is one of the most important figures in the history of the modern NFL," former NBC-TV president Dick Ebersol said. "He and Pete Rozelle developed the magic formula that married the potential of television to the game. Those funds from this marriage propelled the game into what it is today."

Baltimore Orioles owner Peter Angelos called Modell a "visionary" and a "pioneer" in a statement.

Modell owned the Browns for 35 years (1961-1995). During that time, Cleveland qualified for the postseason 17 times and won an NFL championship in 1964. However, financial issues led to Modell relocating the franchise to Baltimore in 1996 and renaming it the Ravens.

The team won the Super Bowl four years later and followed with playoff appearances in two of the next three seasons before Modell sold controlling interest of the Ravens to Steve Bisciotti in 2004.

"He was my friend, my mentor," Bisciotti said. "We will miss him so much. How lucky are all of us to have had Art in Baltimore? How fortunate am I to have had him teach me about the NFL. His generosity, his love, his humor, his intelligence, his friendship — we were all blessed by this great man. We will strive to live up to his standard."

Modell will also be remembered for his charitable work. He donated and raised millions of dollars for many civic and charitable causes. He was on the board of the famed Cleveland Clinic, serving as president of the organization for seven years (1988-95).

He also contributed millions of dollars to a variety of charities in the Baltimore area, including the SEED school, a boarding school for disadvantaged youth, Johns Hopkins hospital, Kennedy Krieger Institute, St. Vincent's center, a home for abused children, and the House of Ruth.

However, for as much as Modell will be remembered for his positive contributions to the NFL, he'll forever be vilified in Cleveland for moving the Browns to Baltimore.

"People still carry a terrible scar and that's understandable," Modell told the *Times* in 2003. "The politicians drove me out of town. The business community took care of the Indians and the Cavaliers, but not the Browns. The memories are unpleasant."

It's a move that has played a significant role in keeping Modell out of the Pro Football Hall of Fame. Modell was one of 15 finalists for the Hall of Fame in

The passing of Art Modell, the Ravens' majority owner until 2003, was in the back of the minds of the Baltimore players during the season.
KEN KOONS/STAFF PHOTO

2001 and has been a semifinalist for classes in 2004, 2005, 2006, 2007, 2009, 2010 and 2011.

"No question the move from Cleveland hurt my possibilities," Modell said. "My record speaks for itself, but obviously the move hurt some people and has hurt me."

Born June 23, 1925, in Brooklyn, N.Y., Arthur B. Modell left high school at the age of 15 to help his financially-troubled family following the death of his father, according to the Ravens.

His first full-time job was as an electrician's helper, cleaning hulls of ships in a Brooklyn shipyard. He joined the Air Force in 1943 at age 18 and then enrolled in television school following World War II, eventually producing "Market Melodies," one of the first regular daytime television shows in the country.

He got into the advertising business in 1954 before purchasing the Browns for $4 million in 1961.

Modell is survived by his sons, John and David, daughter-in-law Michel and six grandchildren. ■

Ravens Seeking One More Game

Team expects no hangover from heartbreaking end to last season

By Matt Zenitz • August 31, 2012

A trip to the Super Bowl looked to be on the verge of being secured. With the Baltimore Ravens trailing the New England Patriots by three in the waning moments of the AFC Championship game in January, quarterback Joe Flacco led a methodical drive, putting the Ravens in position for a late go-ahead score that would all but solidify the Ravens' place in Super Bowl XLVI.

But wide receiver Lee Evans dropped a potential game-winning touchdown, Billy Cundiff shockingly missed a short attempt at a game-tying field goal and for the second time during John Harbaugh's four years as coach, Baltimore was left just a game short of reaching the Super Bowl.

Harbaugh and the Ravens will look to finally take that next step this season, without Evans or Cundiff on the roster.

Asked in May how Baltimore avoids a hangover-like effect considering the disappointing fashion in which last season ended, Harbaugh responded that he doesn't expect it to be a problem.

"I don't think it's an issue," he said. "You go back to work. It's a new season. Our guys, they're in great spirits, so we're excited. We've got lots of things to accomplish, things that we have yet to accomplish."

But if the Ravens are going to accomplish those things, they will need continued progression from Flacco.

He ended the year with an impressive showing in the AFC Championship, but endured an up-and-down 2011 regular season.

He threw for 3,610 yards and 20 touchdowns, his third straight year with at least 3,600 yards and 20 scoring passes, but posted a career-high in turnovers (21) and a career-low in completion percentage (57.6).

Flacco had a strong training camp and preseason, however, looking very much in rhythm with Baltimore's emerging group of young wide receivers and tight ends.

Veteran Anquan Boldin led Baltimore's wideouts in both catches (57) and yards (887) last year while rookie speedster Torrey Smith led the Ravens in touchdown catches (seven).

Smith, a dynamic deep threat, hauled in

Quarterback Joe Flacco has led the Ravens to the playoffs during each of his five seasons.
DYLAN SLAGLE/STAFF PHOTO

50 catches for 841 yards, averaging nearly 17 yards per catch.

He appears poised for an even bigger role heading into his second year.

Free agent pickup Jacoby Jones should also make an impact at wide receiver.

Boldin, Smith and Jones are part of a deep group of capable pass-catchers.

Tight ends Dennis Pitta and Ed Dickson are also expected to play big roles after recovering from pre-season injuries. The two combined for 94 catches and eight touchdowns last season and will be expected to make similar, if not larger contributions this year.

Pro Bowl running back Ray Rice will, obviously, be a primary catalyst for the offense.

The multi-dimensional running back led the NFL in yards from scrimmage last year (2,068), rushing for 1,364 yards and 12 scores while adding a team-high 76 catches for an additional 704 yards and three touchdowns. He has eclipsed 2,000 yards from scrimmage during two of the last three seasons.

"We have to go out there and I think we have to attack," Flacco said, adding the Ravens need to "just become a little bit more accurate, a little bit more pre-cise on everything we do, and I think I start that."

"If we can all get on the same page and all see the defense the same way, we are going to be tough to stop," he continued, "and it's my job to get everyone on the same page and then execute."

What could really shape Baltimore's success this season, however, is how it's able to replace reigning NFL Defensive Player of the Year Terrell Suggs.

Suggs suffered an Achilles tendon injury in May that will sideline him for most of the season and pos-sibly the entire year.

Suggs had an AFC-best 14 sacks and seven forced fumbles last season. With him out, Baltimore has no one on the roster that has ever recorded more than six sacks in a season.

The sense of urgency to replace Suggs is made even greater by the long list of talented quarter-backs the Ravens face this year, including Michael Vick, Tom Brady, Tony Romo, Matt Schaub, Ben Roethlisberger, Philip Rivers, Peyton Manning and Eli Manning.

Asked in May whether he was confident the Ravens could withstand the loss of Suggs, Harbaugh said, "Of course."

"It's obvious," he said. "It's a team. We're a team. That's why you draft guys and bring guys in. It's never about one guy, ever.

"We've handled losses to our biggest stars, now Terrell, Ray [Lewis] and Ed [Reed]. That's all hap-pened in the last two years. It will be up to all of us to do a little bit better, and we intend to improve in anything we do, including our defense." ■

Opposite: Originally signed as an undrafted free agent, linebacker Jameel McClain has emerged as a key contributor on defense, the Ravens' hallmark for years. Above: Vonta Leach, one of the game's best run-blocking fullbacks, spikes the ball in celebration after scoring a touchdown during a preseason game against Jacksonville. DYLAN SLAGLE/STAFF PHOTO

REGULAR SEASON • SEPTEMBER 10, 2012

Baltimore, Maryland • Ravens 44, Bengals 13

Opening Statement

Flacco, offense impressive in blowout of Bengals

By Matt Zenitz

It was a performance that had Baltimore Ravens coach John Harbaugh proclaiming afterward that quarterback Joe Flacco could be "scary good" this season.

Flacco showed glimpses of being on the brink of a potentially special season during training camp and the preseason, but his performance during the Ravens' 44-13 season-opening blowout of the Cincinnati Bengals served as an even bigger indication.

Flacco was near flawless in the win, throwing for 299 yards and two touchdowns while completing 21 of his 29 pass attempts.

"Scary good. That's the probably the word right there," a passionate Harbaugh stated when asked how good Flacco could be this season.

Making it look almost easy, Flacco picked apart an overmatched Bengals secondary, spreading the ball around to his bevy of options as he guided Baltimore to points on six of its first seven possessions.

"This is what we've seen [from Flacco] all of camp with Joe just throwing the ball to those guys, putting it right in their chest, putting it right in their hands," Ravens safety Ed Reed said, later adding, "Like I've been saying the whole time since Joe's been here, he's been our guy. He's been making plays, making throws that everybody else across the league isn't making."

Operating out of the same no-huddle, up-tempo offense that was so prevalent during both training camp and the preseason, Flacco came out firing Monday night.

He hooked up with second-year speedster Torrey Smith for a 52-yard gain on Baltimore's first play from scrimmage, one of seven passing plays of 18 yards or more for Flacco.

The Ravens racked up 430 yards of total offense.

"We didn't get that many drives, really, but we were efficient enough that we put points on the board," Flacco said.

Yet, Cincinnati hung around through the early part of the second half.

The Bengals trailed just 17-13 midway through the third quarter before Flacco capped a nine-play, 89-yard drive with a

Quarterback Joe Flacco threw for 299 yards and two touchdowns during the Ravens' blowout win over Cincinnati on *Monday Night Football*. DYLAN SLAGLE/STAFF PHOTO

10-yard touchdown pass to tight end Dennis Pitta.

The game quickly spiraled out of control from there.

Cincinnati followed with a three-and-out. And after a 40-yard field goal from Baltimore kicker Justin Tucker, Bengals quarterback Andy Dalton tossed an interception on the third play of Cincinnati's ensuing drive that Ravens safety Ed Reed returned 34 yards for a touchdown to push Baltimore's advantage to 34-13 with 13 seconds left in the third quarter.

Dalton coughed up a fumble on the third play of the Bengals' next possession, giving the Ravens' offense possession at Cincinnati's 28-yard line. They capitalized with a 1-yard Ray Rice scoring run just three plays later.

"It was no question that we left some plays out there," Bengals running back Benjarvus Green-Ellis said. "We went into halftime with some momentum.... We did some good things, but it just wasn't enough. Hats off to the Ravens. They came out and played really well. They were ready to play and we need to play better."

Green-Ellis had some success on the ground, rushing for 91 yards on 18 carries, but carried the ball just twice following Cincinnati's first drive of the second half as Baltimore built its lead.

Dalton threw for 221 yards, but didn't have much success down the field and most of his damage was done on underneath routes and bubble screens to wide receiver Andrew Hawkins.

The speedy and elusive Hawkins led the Bengals with eight catches for 86 yards.

After struggling to generate a pass rush during the first half, the Ravens' defense did a better job getting to Dalton in the second, eventually finishing with four sacks.

"I think we did very good," Baltimore defensive lineman Pernell McPhee said of the Ravens' defensive effort. "I think we had our miscues in the first half, but came in and at halftime and fixed some things and came out the second half and shut them down." ■

One of the NFL's best deep ball passers, quarterback Joe Flacco prepares to throw against the Bengals. DYLAN SLAGLE/STAFF PHOTO

Ravens Fall In Philly

Offense struggles as Eagles erase 10-point halftime deficit

By Matt Zenitz

Baltimore Ravens quarterback Joe Flacco immediately threw his hands to the air in frustration following the Ravens' failed fourth down attempt late in the fourth quarter, leaving them there for a few moments while staring in the direction of the play almost in relative disbelief.

The reaction wasn't as much for anything that transpired on that particular play as much as it was a culmination of a mistake-filled day for Flacco and the Ravens' offense amid Baltimore's 24-23 loss to the Philadelphia Eagles Sunday afternoon at Lincoln Financial Field.

Just six days earlier, Flacco and Baltimore's offense could seemingly do no wrong.

Sunday was a different story.

Matched up against one of the NFL's top defenses, Flacco and the offense struggled for most of the second half as the Ravens allowed a 17-7 halftime lead to slip away in suffering their first loss of the season.

"I just think they did a good job all day of just coming up there and putting enough guys in the box and putting pressure on our receivers," Flacco said. "They've got two good corners that it's

tough to consistently do a lot of damage on those guys. And they've got a good pass rush up front, so we had to get the ball out of our hands quickly."

Less than a week after his standout performance against the Cincinnati Bengals, Flacco was just 22-of-42 for 232 yards with a touchdown and an interception. He was 8-of-25 with an interception during the second half.

Baltimore held a 10-point advantage at halftime, but had an interception and three three-and-outs on its first four possessions of the second half just as Michael Vick and the Eagles' offense were beginning to have prolonged success against the Ravens' defense.

Vick led three second half scoring drives, including one in the final minutes that he capped with a 1-yard scoring run to give Philadelphia a 24-23 advantage with 1:55 left in the fourth quarter.

Baltimore had a chance to counter with a go-ahead scoring drive of its own, but sputtered after moving the ball near midfield.

Flacco completed a 9-yard pass to tight end Dennis Pitta to advance the ball to the Ravens' 46-yard line, but he followed with incomplete passes on both third-and-1 and fourth-and-1 to turn the ball over on downs.

The Eagles ran out the clock from there.

Philadelphia outgained Baltimore 264-146 during the second half.

"Obviously we gave up more than we scored," Ravens coach John Harbaugh said. "That's not what we want to do. We want to give up less than we scored. That's the idea. That's team football. That's how we look at it, all three phases.... So I'm disappointed in all three phases because we weren't able to find a way to win in that sense."

Vick finished 23-of-32 for 371 yards with one touchdown and two interceptions.

He added 34 yards and a score on the ground.

Tight end Brent Celek was Vick's top target, consistently exploiting Baltimore when it went to zone coverage. He hauled in eight catches for 157 yards, averaging nearly 20 yards per catch.

Philadelphia produced nine plays of 19 yards or more through the air.

"They just caught us," Baltimore cornerback Cary Williams said. "They were the better team today and were able to finish. We just didn't get it done."

Trailing 23-17 with 4:43 left in the fourth quarter, Vick guided the Eagles on a 10-play, 80-yard drive that he finished with his 1-yard touchdown run.

Philadelphia actually had some success moving the ball in the first half as well, but came away with just seven points as a result of three first half turnovers, all of which came inside the Ravens' 20-yard line.

Vick marched the Eagles down the field on their first possession of the game, advancing the ball to Baltimore's 13-yard line before he tried to force a pass in the end zone to tight end Clay Harbor and was intercepted by Ravens safety Bernard Pollard.

Flacco fumbled two plays later to give Philadelphia the ball back at Baltimore's 20-yard line and the Eagles took advantage with a 2-yard scoring run by running back LeSean McCoy.

McCoy had the touchdown, but was limited to

Quarterback Joe Flacco, who threw for 232 yards during the 24-23 defeat, launches a pass against the Eagles. AP Images

only 81 yards on 25 carries as Ravens outside linebackers Albert McClellan and Courtney Upshaw did a good job preventing McCoy from breaking any big runs to the outside.

McClellan and Upshaw both recorded six tackles.

The Ravens answered Philadelphia's opening score with a touchdown run of its own as fullback Vonta Leach bulled in from five yards out on Baltimore's ensuing possession.

Ravens running back Ray Rice broke off a 43-yard run two drives later to set up Flacco's 21-yard touchdown pass to wide receiver Jacoby Jones five minutes into the second quarter.

Rookie kicker Justin Tucker extended Baltimore's lead to 17-7 with a team-record tying 56-yard field goal with one second left in the first half.

The field goal was one of three for Tucker, who was 3-of-3 on the afternoon. All three of his makes were from 48 yards or beyond, including his 51-yard kick early in the fourth quarter after the Eagles had tied the score at 17.

He added a 48-yard field goal on the Ravens' next possession, but Vick followed by leading Philadelphia down the field for the go-ahead score in the final minutes. ■

REGULAR SEASON • SEPTEMBER 23, 2012
Baltimore, Maryland • Ravens 31, Patriots 30

Flacco Rallies Ravens

Tucker, Smith Step Up in the Clutch
By Matt Zenitz

It was an eerily similar finish to the AFC championship just eight months earlier.

The only difference — this time the Ravens' kicker didn't miss on a potentially crucial kick.

After a methodical last-minute drive by Joe Flacco and Baltimore's offense — similar to the one Flacco engineered against the New England Patriots in the AFC title game the previous January — rookie kicker Justin Tucker connected on a 27-yard field goal as time expired to propel the Ravens to a dramatic 31-30 win against the Patriots Sunday night.

In January, then-Baltimore kicker Billy Cundiff missed on a 32-yard field goal in the waning moments of the AFC title game, ending the Ravens' season and propelling New England to the Super Bowl.

It was the first pressure kick for Tucker, the rookie from Texas who unseated Cundiff during training camp, and the rookie delivered.

Overcoming a bad snap, Tucker split the uprights as time expired.

His kick appeared to be tailing wide right, but barely snuck inside the right upright.

"It's big, really big," Baltimore coach John Harbaugh said of Tucker, who's now 7-of-7 on field goals this season. "To be the first game-winner like that I think it's something every kicker would cherish."

Flacco finished 28-of-39 for 382 yards with three touchdowns and one interception, overcoming a slow start to help the Ravens erase an early 13-0 deficit.

His third scoring pass — a 5-yarder to wide receiver Torrey Smith — trimmed New England's advantage to 30-28 with 4:01 left in the fourth quarter.

And after Baltimore forced a punt on the Patriots' next drive, giving the Ravens the ball back at their own 21-yard line with 1:55 remaining, Flacco led an 8-play, 70-yard drive that put Baltimore in position for Tucker's game-winning kick.

Flacco and the Ravens' offense rebounded from a less than ideal start.

New England outgained Baltimore 143-21 during the first quarter, a quarter during which Flacco was just 3-of-5 for a meager 10 yards with an interception.

Linebacker Ray Lewis fires up his team before the Ravens' Sept. 23 face-off against the New England Patriots, the team the Ravens later met in the AFC Championship Game. DYLAN SLAGLE/STAFF PHOTO

The Ravens failed to pick up a first down during the opening quarter as the Patriots jumped out to a quick 13-0 lead.

But Flacco and the offense came to life from there, aided by the play of Smith, who played Sunday night even despite the death of his little brother less than 24 hours earlier.

Smith hauled in six catches for 127 yards and two scores.

His 25-yard touchdown catch early in the second quarter capped a 13-play, 80-yard drive that cut New England's advantage to 13-7.

Flacco hooked up with tight end Dennis Pitta on a 20-yard score on Baltimore's next possession, but Tom Brady responded by leading a long drive of his own which he capped with a 7-yard touchdown to Julian Edelman just two seconds before the end of the first half.

The two teams traded scores early in the third quarter before Stephen Gostkowski's field goal pushed the Patriots' advantage to 30-21 less than a minute into the fourth quarter.

New England followed by stopping the Ravens on a fourth-and-1 on their ensuing possession. But after Baltimore's defense came up with a stop of its own, Flacco guided a Ravens scoring drive that ended with his second touchdown pass to Smith.

Flacco was 25-of-34 for 372 yards and three scores during the final three quarters.

"I just thought it was fantastic," Harbaugh said. "It was elite. It's who Joe is. It's who he's always been."

The Ravens' defense struggled to slow down Brady and the Patriots' passing game, but came up with two big stops during the fourth quarter, including the one that gave Baltimore's offense the ball back with a chance for the game-winning score.

Brady finished 28-of-41 for 335 yards with one touchdown and no interceptions.

"Couldn't be more proud of this football team," Harbaugh said, later adding, "I hope that's who we are, hope that's how we're defined. I hope we don't have to do it this way all the time, though." ■

Joe Flacco finished 28-of-39 for 382 yards and with three touchdown passes as the Ravens overcame a slow start to defeat the Patriots.
DYLAN SLAGLE/STAFF PHOTO

HEAD COACH

John Harbaugh

Ravens title run five years in the making

By Matt Zenitz • February 3, 2013

Ray Lewis talked Thursday about a brief period of reminiscing he shared with safety Ed Reed during Wednesday's practice. The two thought back on the last decade. They reflected on all of the years the Ravens fell just short of the point they find themselves now. They talked about all of the great defenses gone to waste. They thought back on the close calls, the bitter season-ending defeats and the team's overall inability to find a way to advance to the NFL's championship game.

And they talked about how special this year's run has been — a run that has Baltimore back in the Super Bowl for the first time since winning Super Bowl XXXV during the 2000 season.

It's a trip that's really been five years in the making under head coach John Harbaugh — a five-year journey that's seen the Ravens' offense, in particular quarterback Joe Flacco, progressing to the point to lead Baltimore on this exact kind of run.

Harbaugh, Flacco and running back Ray Rice all arrived in Baltimore in 2008. The five years that followed have included 54 regular season wins, five trips to the playoffs, three trips to the AFC title game and now the Ravens' first Super Bowl appearance in more than a decade.

"We've been close," Lewis said. "We've been close many, many years. But, I've always said that one play, one catch or one missed field goal — whatever it is — has never defined a season. I just believe that whatever time that expires during the course of that year, it expires.

"Now, you saw a lot of bounces of the ball went our way. A lot of things in the last couple of games, they just went our way. Positive energy comes into play with that. By the end of day, I just think that if it is your time, it's your time. For us to be here today, it's, bottom line, our time."

But where did this come from?

Yes, the Ravens have been great in the playoffs. Their offense is surging behind the play of Flacco. And their defense has fared well against three high-powered offenses.

But this is the same team that less than two months ago was mired in a three-game losing streak. Their offense was sputtering, in particular Flacco and the passing game. And their defense, decimated by injuries, was struggling against both the run and the pass.

At the time, they looked little like a team capable of contending for a Super Bowl.

Yet, exactly two months to the day after it suffered a lopsided loss to the Denver Broncos, Baltimore now finds itself just a win over the San Francisco 49ers away from a Super Bowl title.

"We've gone through a lot this year," Ravens tight end Dennis Pitta said. "We've had a lot of adversity, a lot of highs and lows. It's been a tremendous year. We've had a lot to overcome to

Coach John Harbaugh, who has won at least one playoff game during each of his five years in Baltimore, commands his team during a loss to the Texans. AP Images

get to this point. It's been a long journey."

They're a team that's dealt with the death of former majority owner Art Modell. There was the death of wide receiver Torrey Smith's younger brother. There were the numerous injuries to key defensive players that had Baltimore's traditionally stout defense looking very much vulnerable during much of the regular season. There were the struggles on offense, especially within the passing game, that led to the firing of offensive coordinator Cam Cameron. And there was the three-game losing streak late in the regular season that had most on a national level doubting how much of a threat Baltimore would be come playoff time.

"That's what made the journey — the adversity," Harbaugh said, later adding, "You can go with so many guys who have so many things going on this year that were personal, and then obviously the football stuff, too. It's a professional livelihood and they fight through things — the wins and the losses and all that stuff.

"And the criticism, and all that, it's all part of it. We all take it personal. It's who we are. So, it either tears you apart or pushes you together. And it pushed our team together."

But it's been an improbable, unexplainable and storybook season in so many ways for the Ravens.

Even aside from the sudden turnaround that has them now on the cusp of a Super Bowl title, there was Ray Rice's fourth-and-29 conversion against the San Diego Chargers in mid-November and Flacco's game-tying 70-yard touchdown pass to Jacoby Jones with Baltimore trailing the Broncos by seven points in the divisional round of the playoffs with less than a minute remaining in the fourth quarter and the Ravens facing a third-and-3 at their own 30-yard line without a single timeout.

A week after beating the Broncos, Baltimore completed its journey to the Super Bowl with a win over the New England Patriots at Gillette Stadium in Foxborough, almost a year to the day that the Ravens fell to the Patriots at Gillette Stadium in last season's AFC title game.

"The difference between this team and other teams is that we got the job done when it needed to get done," Ravens tight end Ed Dickson said. "We honed in and focused when we needed to focus. We didn't win every game ... but you're going to have your ups and downs, your triumphs and your failures. You're going to have those.

"It's how you battle back from those things, and how you learn from your losses.... You've got to improve in everything that you do, and that's just the major difference with this team and every other team that I've played for with the Ravens."

And it's something players say they've been able to do behind the guidance of Harbaugh.

"He's just a really tough guy," Baltimore cornerback Cary Williams said of Harbaugh, later adding, "He's just an unbelievable coach, an unbelievable mentor to a lot of guys and just an uplifting spirit in the locker room. He's definitely gritty."

Harbaugh was hired by the Ravens in 2008, inheriting a team that went 5-11 the year before, but he's led Baltimore to a 54-26 record during the five regular seasons that have followed and another eight wins in the playoffs.

"He pushes us to the limit," Baltimore outside linebacker Albert McClellan said of Harbaugh. "We've been strong the last few years. Now, we just need to find a way to get this [win]. Once we do, he's probably going to be viewed as one of the best coaches in the league."

Harbaugh's brother, 49ers coach Jim Harbaugh, told CSN Bay Area last month that John "is the best in the league at what he does."

Said Jim: "I don't think there's any coach coaching in the game today that really has the full grasp of offense, defense and special teams like [John] has."

And now, led by John, the Ravens are just a win over Jim's 49ers away from the second Super Bowl title in franchise history.

Said cornerback Cary Williams: "One of our goals was to get to the Super Bowl, but we still have one goal left, and that's to win the Super Bowl, so we're going to keep our eye on the prize." ■

Head coach John Harbaugh talks to reporters on July 24, 2012, the day of the Ravens' first training camp practice. DYLAN SLAGLE/STAFF PHOTO

REGULAR SEASON • SEPTEMBER 27, 2012

Baltimore, Maryland • Ravens 23, Browns 16

Ravens' Pressure Prevails

Williams bounces back, proves to be "the difference" in Thursday night victory

By Matt Zenitz

By the time Cleveland Browns receiver Travis Benjamin cut his route toward the sideline, Baltimore Ravens cornerback Cary Williams had already begun his break for the ball.

Recognizing the situation — a third-and-4 — Williams anticipated Benjamin's short out route, hopped in front and intercepted Brandon Weeden's attempted pass for Benjamin before racing down the sideline for what proved to be a critical 63-yard touchdown return amid the Ravens' 23-16 Thursday night.

The interception came at a key moment for Baltimore, providing cushion after Cleveland had trimmed its deficit to 16-10 late in the third quarter.

Just days earlier, Williams was the subject of substantial criticism after struggling during Sunday's win against the New England Patriots.

Thursday, however, Baltimore coach John Harbaugh referred to Williams as "the difference in the game."

"Here is a guy who was under a lot of heat from [the media]," Harbaugh said. "But he wasn't under heat in our building because we know what kind of player he is, and he came up big."

Fellow Ravens cornerback Lardarius Webb described Williams' interception as "a huge moment."

"They kept messing with him," Webb said of the Browns' offense. "But we knew that he would eventually come through. I've been working with him every day since training camp, and I know what he's got. He started off a little slow, but you see the big play potential in him. He makes plays and that's why we believe in him."

The Browns battled back, though.

Two fourth-quarter Phil Dawson field goals cut the Ravens' advantage to 23-16. And after Cleveland's defense forced a Baltimore punt with just more than a minute remaining in the fourth quarter, Weeden led the Browns into position for a game-tying score.

Ravens rookie offensive lineman Kelechi Osemele keeps Browns defensive end Jabaal Sheard away from quarterback Joe Flacco. DYLAN SLAGLE/STAFF PHOTO

But after guiding Cleveland's offense to the Ravens' 18-yard line in the waning moments of the quarter, Weeden's attempt at a game-tying touchdown pass sailed out of the end zone as time expired amid pressure from the Baltimore's defensive line.

The Ravens had stopped the Browns on fourth down a play earlier, but a personal foul on Baltimore outside linebacker Paul Kruger gave Cleveland one more shot at the end zone.

"Once we got through it, it was like, 'Oh, finally,'" Webb said. "But it's nice to have the game on our [defense's] back. We really stepped up when we had to. We did a great job getting them off the field. We had a crazy call at the end. But still, that adversity we faced it and we won the game."

Weeden threw for 320 yards, but completed just 25 of his 52 pass attempts and was without a touchdown.

With the Ravens employing a variety of blitz packages aimed to confuse the rookie quarterback, Weeden was under constant pressure.

Baltimore had just one sack, but recorded eight quarterback hits.

Kruger had the Ravens' lone sack, but middle linebackers Ray Lewis and Jameel McClain also generated pressure as pass rushers, as did defensive linemen Pernell McPhee and Haloti Ngata.

Five of Cleveland's six second half possessions extended into Baltimore territory, but the five drives produced a total of just nine points.

The Browns were 3-of-15 on third down.

Cleveland rookie running back Trent Richardson was limited to 47 yards on 14 carries, but added 57 yards on four catches and had a 1-yard scoring run late in the second quarter that sent the Browns into halftime trailing just 9-7.

"It's just one or two plays, that's the difference," Browns offensive tackle Joe Thomas said.

Baltimore outgained Cleveland 438-357.

Despite constant pressure from an aggressive Browns defense, Ravens quarterback Joe Flacco finished 28-of-46 for 356 yards with one touchdown and one interception.

Flacco was sacked a season-high four times, and hit several more times, but delivered several big throws down the field.

Wide receiver Anquan Boldin led Baltimore with nine catches for 131 yards.

He had three grabs for 60 yards during the Ravens' first drive of the third quarter, helping set up a 1-yard Flacco scoring run that pushed Baltimore's lead to 16-7.

He also had a key 28-yard catch late in the fourth quarter, making an acrobatic grab over Cleveland cornerback Dimitri Patterson, with the Ravens leading by seven and just less than four minutes remaining.

"Anquan Boldin had some huge catches for us, especially that conversion down there on the sideline," Harbaugh said.

Torrey Smith had 97 yards on six catches for Baltimore, including an 18-yard touchdown that opened the scoring early in the second quarter.

Ravens running back Ray Rice was held in check on the ground, limited to 49 yards on 18 carries, but was effective as a receiver out of the backfield. He had eight catches for 47 yards.

Thursday's game marked Baltimore's fourth in an 18-day span to start the season, but the team will now have some time for recovery prior to traveling to face the Kansas City Chiefs Oct. 7.

"I'm tired, man," Rice joked. "I can't wait to have this weekend off." ▪

Running back Ray Rice, who carried for 49 yards during the Thursday night contest, rumbles through the Browns defense. DYLAN SLAGLE/STAFF PHOTO

Kansas City, Missouri • Ravens 9, Chiefs 6

Defensive Dominance

Ravens escape Kansas City with "ugly" victory

By Matt Zenitz

It was a rough day for the Baltimore Ravens' offense.

Quarterback Joe Flacco completed less than 50 percent of his passes, receivers struggled to get open against a physical Kansas City Chiefs secondary and the Ravens' offensive line surrendered consistent pressure to Kansas City's talented pass rush tandem of Tamba Hali and Justin Houston.

Fortunately for Baltimore, it was an even rougher day for the Chiefs' offense.

And capitalizing on four Kansas City turnovers, including one that came on a first-and-goal from the Ravens' 1-yard line, Baltimore escaped Arrowhead Stadium with what Ravens safety Bernard Pollard acknowledged was an "ugly" 9-6 victory Sunday afternoon.

It was exactly five years to the day since the last time Baltimore (4-1) had won without scoring a single touchdown, the previous time being the Ravens' 9-7 win against the San Francisco 49ers Oct. 7, 2007.

"There is such a thing as an ugly victory," Pollard said. "You're not going to blow everyone out all the time. You're not going to dominate all the time. You're going to come to the point where it's a dogfight, and today was a dogfight."

Flacco finished just 13-of-27 for 187 yards with no touchdowns and one interception.

He was sacked four times — twice each by Hali and Houston.

Hali's second sack appeared to result in a Flacco fumble, which Kansas City (1-4) would have recovered in the end zone for a go-ahead touchdown in the final minutes of the fourth quarter, but referees whistled the play dead prior to the fumble.

So rather than a Chiefs touchdown, the Ravens retained the ball as well as their three-point lead. They picked up a first down on the next play, picked up another three plays later and proceeded to run out the clock.

Baltimore was just 3-of-11 on third down conversions, but picked up two on that final drive of the fourth quarter.

"It feels good to win the game," Flacco said. "That was just part of what

Veteran center Matt Birk paves the way for quarterback Joe Flacco during the Ravens' hard-fought win over the Chiefs, in which the teams combined for just 15 points. AP Images

we had to do to win the game. They're not always pretty around here, but there's one thing we do around here — we do what we have to do to win the football game.

"I've been saying that for a long time, whether that's throwing for 400 yards or having a crap day and throwing for 100 yards," Flacco added. "We do what we have to do to win the game and we were able to do that [today]."

Anquan Boldin led Baltimore with 82 yards on four catches, but had two uncharacteristic drops during the first half.

Ravens pass catchers had five drops Sunday, most of which came during a first half that ended with the score tied at 3.

Baltimore was outgained 338-298 Sunday, including 216-106 in the first half.

The Ravens picked up just six first downs during the first half.

"They played well," Flacco said of Kansas City's defense. "I think they're a good defense.... We weren't able to keep those guys on the field. We weren't able to convert. We never really got into a rhythm in the first half. They contested catches, contested passes."

The Chiefs' offense, meanwhile, had success moving the ball against Baltimore's defense.

Kansas City running back Jamaal Charles was limited to just 15 yards on 10 carries during the second half, but finished with 140 yards on 30 carries.

As a team, the Chiefs, intent on running the ball, picked up 214 yards on 50 carries.

They threw the ball only 18 times.

Kansas City ran the ball 34 times during the first half while attempting just seven passes. The 34 runs tied the 2009 New York Jets for the most first-half rushing attempts by any team in the last 20 seasons.

Much-maligned quarterback Matt Cassel was 9-of-15 for 92 yards with two interceptions prior to exiting with a head injury during the fourth quarter.

"Our plan was to go in and try to slow down the game," Charles said. "We were trying to get the ball in my hands and the other running backs' hands."

And the Chiefs had success doing so, especially during the first half. But as has been the case all season for Kansas City's offense, it was derailed by turnovers.

Eight of the Chiefs' 11 possessions stretched into Ravens territory, but Kansas City managed just two Ryan Succop field goals.

Three of the Chiefs' four turnovers came inside Baltimore's 40-yard line, including a botched handoff between Cassel and center Ryan Lilja on a first-and-goal from the Ravens' 1-yard line that Baltimore safety Ed Reed recovered in the end zone to prevent Kansas City from taking the lead early in the second half.

The Ravens' offense followed with a 7-play, 80-yard drive that ended with a 26-yard Justin Tucker field goal. The kick gave Baltimore a 6-3 lead midway through the third quarter.

"That was big, obviously," Baltimore coach John Harbaugh said. "That ended up being a 10-point swing. It was huge.... It was important in the football game."

Tucker added another short field goal later in the quarter. But after Kansas City forced a three-and-out on the Ravens' next possession, the Chiefs drove for what looked to be a go-ahead touchdown as backup quarterback Brady Quinn, in for the injured Cassel, hooked up with wide receiver Dwayne Bowe for an apparent 15-yard scoring pass.

But Kansas City was flagged for offensive pass interference on the play, negating the touchdown and forcing the Chiefs to settle for a Succop field goal.

Kansas City's offense never got the ball back.

"The ones that count are never the prettiest," Baltimore linebacker Ray Lewis said. "The ones that count the most are the ones that you have to fight through. Anybody on each side of the ball will tell you that they'll take a 'W' before anything. For us to go home right now 4-1 is huge." ■

Ravens rookie kicker Justin Tucker, who was responsible for all of the Ravens' points on the day, kicks a field goal through the uprights. AP Images

REGULAR SEASON • OCTOBER 14, 2012

Baltimore, Maryland • Ravens 31, Cowboys 29

Ravens Wrangle Wild Win

Dallas missed field goal clinches Baltimore victory

By Matt Zenitz

Ravens cornerback Cary Williams jumped in jubilation before excitedly sprinting toward Baltimore's sideline.

Dallas Cowboys kicker Dan Bailey had just missed on an attempt at a game-winning field goal, capping a wild final 36 seconds and allowing the Ravens to escape with a 31-29 victory Sunday afternoon.

"I was happy as hell," Williams said while smiling, later adding, "I'm happy. I'm ecstatic. This is a great win for the organization. As far as I'm concerned, I'm going to smile all night."

Bailey's miss was the culmination of a crazy finish Sunday.

Less than a minute earlier, the Ravens came up with what looked to be a game-deciding stop on a Dallas two-point conversion attempt. Yet, just moments later, the Cowboys had new life after recovering an onside kick. And after a pass interference penalty on Baltimore cornerback Chykie Brown advanced the ball to the Ravens' 34-yard line, the Cowboys appeared to be in range for a Bailey field goal.

But after a short-gain on their next play, Bailey missed left and the Ravens (5-1) salvaged the win.

"I'm just proud of this team," Baltimore coach John Harbaugh said. "It was a team victory. Was it perfect? Was it pretty? No. And I'm sure that's all stuff that will get written about, and it's all fine, but a victory is still a victory."

Baltimore was once again gashed on the ground — the second straight week that's happened — but Ravens quarterback Joe Flacco had success against a Dallas pass-defense that entered Sunday as the NFL's best.

The Cowboys (2-3) limited their first four opponents to an average of just 169.5 yards per game, but Flacco finished 17-of-26 for 234 yards with one touchdown and no interceptions.

Exploiting the same press-man coverage that gave Baltimore's passing game trouble just a week earlier, Flacco completed passes to eight different receivers.

Anquan Boldin led the Ravens with five catches for 98 yards. Torrey Smith

Special teams ace Jacoby Jones returns a third-quarter kickoff 109 yards for a touchdown.
DYLAN SLAGLE/STAFF PHOTO

had two catches for 24 yards, including a 19-yard touchdown to give Baltimore a 17-10 lead late in the second quarter.

"We just ran our offense," Smith said. "There's nothing special about press-man. I'm so glad we were able to move the ball so you all [the media] could stop asking us about press-man, but we were able to finish and make enough plays. We lucked out — got a little bit of luck — but the offense made enough plays and we've just got some work to do as a team."

With its running game as the catalyst, Dallas outgained the Ravens 481-316 and held a significant edge in time of possession (40:03 to 19:57).

After struggling to establish their rushing attack in recent weeks, the Cowboys racked up 227 yards on 42 carries while averaging more than five yards per carry.

The 227 rushing yards represent the most-ever allowed by Baltimore.

Dallas running back DeMarco Murray had 13 carries for 90 yards during the first half, but missed most of the second half with a sprained foot, giving way to backup Felix Jones. Jones finished with 92 yards on 18 carries. The Cowboys even had some success with third-stringer Phillip Tanner (nine carries for 31 yards) and fourth-stringer Lance Dunbar (one carry for 11 yards).

"They did a good job running the ball — finding holes, finding seams," Ravens defensive lineman Arthur Jones said, later adding, "We've got to do a better job wrapping up and tackling."

Dallas threw the ball nearly 70 percent of the time during its first four games, but employed a run-first approach Sunday.

The Ravens have yielded 441 rushing yards during their last two games. They surrendered 214 yards on 50 carries against the Kansas City Chiefs last week.

"I thought we did a good job with [our running game],"Cowboys coach Jason Garrett said. "We stayed after them. We ran it inside, we ran it outside. We got some good stuff out of the run games and I thought that was a positive for us."

Dallas quarterback Tony Romo was 25-of-36 for 261 yards with two touchdowns and one interception.

He struggled early — going just 9-of-12 for 81 yards with no touchdowns and the interception during the first half — but had some success late against a pass defense that was without top cornerback Lardarius Webb.

Webb suffered a potential season-ending knee injury during the second quarter.

Romo was 16-of-24 for 180 yards with two scores and no interceptions in the second half.

Wide receiver Dez Bryant had 13 catches for 95 yards and two scores.

His second touchdown, a 4-yard grab, trimmed Baltimore's advantage to 31-29 with 36 seconds remaining in the fourth quarter, but he followed by dropping what would've been a game-tying two-point conversion.

Dallas recovered an onside kick moments later, but Bailey missed on the game-winning field goal attempt with seconds left in the quarter.

"We have things that need to be fixed, and we're going to go ahead and do that, but most importantly we got the win," Jones said. "That's what it comes

Quarterback Joe Flacco, who completed 17 of his 26 passes for 234 yards and a touchdown against the Cowboys, prepares to throw during the second half. DYLAN SLAGLE/STAFF PHOTO

52

LINEBACKER

Ray Lewis

Ravens make a run for Ray

By Bob Blubaugh • January 6, 2013

The main wall in an old-school Carroll County barber shop is adorned by exactly one autographed photo of a Baltimore Raven. It's Ray Lewis. A few feet away hangs a Ray Lewis Ravens cap.

The customer in one of the chairs is getting a haircut from a shear expert wearing Lewis' No. 52 Ravens jersey, one of thousands across the state decked out in that fashion on this so-called "purple Friday."

Perhaps more remarkable than all his tackles, Pro Bowl appearances and awards is the fact that Lewis — a reviled figure early in his career who accepted a misdemeanor obstruction plea after being charged with murder — became the most beloved of all Ravens as well as a popular player nationally. A glib pitchman, he will take his powerful personality to ESPN once this season ends.

His passion, his religious fervor for the game, has always resonated.

As much as fans like Lewis and respect his game, however, it doesn't compare to the way those who really know him feel about him. Teammates past and present have been effusive in their praise of the embodiment of Ravens football since his Wednesday announcement

that he will retire at the end of this, his 17th season in the NFL.

Oh, it will be a highly motivated Baltimore football team that takes the field today against the Indianapolis Colts in the first round of the playoffs. Lewis' teammates have vowed to do everything they can to help the future Hall of Famer go out on top.

"We will give all we've got Sunday for Ray. We owe it to him," running back Ray Rice told reporters on Wednesday. "I don't want it to be the last time I play with him."

How far can emotion and inspiration take a team? Pretty far. Just look at the other team on the field today.

With a talent level near the bottom of the league one year after going 2-14, the Colts were universally expected to stink. And they lost two of three to start before their coach, Chuck Pagano, was diagnosed with leukemia. Inspired by "Chuckstrong," rookie quarterback Andrew Luck and the Colts became the surprise story of the season, going 11-5 and making the postseason.

Still, this is a great matchup for a Ravens team that struggled to 1-4 in December. Rice & Co. should be able to run all over Indy. Ed Reed is the last safety a young QB wants to throw

A 17-year veteran, linebacker Ray Lewis remained as intense and fiery as ever during his final season. DYLAN SLAGLE/STAFF PHOTO

against. And Lewis' fresh legs in his first game since tearing his triceps in Week 6 were expected to be an asset even before his surprise announcement.

Not that a team needs extra motivation in the playoffs, but the Ravens now have it. As hard as Lewis worked to get back from his injury, as much as he has meant to the franchise since the day he was drafted in 1996, what player or coach would dare give anything less than maximum effort?

Those who've watched him and studied him over the years are calling him one of the best — if not the best — middle linebackers in history. Those who've played alongside him are calling him the best — not one of the best — teammate they ever had.

Trent Dilfer, who parlayed half-a-season as a starting quarterback in Baltimore into a championship ring, a Disney trip that should've gone to Super Bowl XXXV MVP Lewis, and a career as an ESPN analyst, spent only one of his 13 years in the NFL as Lewis' teammate. That was enough for him to know all he needed to about "God's Linebacker," who impressed Dilfer as much off the field as on.

"He is the most productive player but his messaging within the locker room is always right," Dilfer said this week. "You trust everything about him and he makes everybody better.... There's an intensity to him. That intensity is authentic. It's genuine and it's always directed at making the football organization better.

"I've never seen a person better than him at those three layers: preparation, leadership and play."

Lewis has been preparing for this game for three months. And his entire life.

Seeing him emerge from the tunnel for one last pregame dance will be unforgettable. For fans, for players, for Lewis himself.

"That moment is for everybody from the day I walked in here in 1996," Lewis said Wednesday. "It will be probably one of the glorious moments of my life." ■

As became a tradition before home games at M&T Bank Stadium, linebacker Ray Lewis pumps up both his teammates and the home crowd. DYLAN SLAGLE/

REGULAR SEASON • OCTOBER 21, 2012

Houston, Texas • Texans 43, Ravens 13

Texas Tumble

Ravens suffer worst defeat of Harbaugh era

By Matt Zenitz

Joe Flacco had one of the worst statistical performances of his career, the Ravens' offensive line struggled against the Houston Texans' front seven and Baltimore's defense surrendered the most points during John Harbaugh's five years as head coach.

Not much went well for the Ravens amid Sunday's 43-13 loss to Houston.

The margin of defeat was Baltimore's largest since falling to the Pittsburgh Steelers, 38-7, Nov. 5, 2007, during the season preceding Harbaugh taking over as head coach.

"Not much to say about that other than they got after us and they beat us," Harbaugh said. "Give them credit. They played excellent and we did not. That's what happens on the road against a good team. We'll have to regroup and get back and play a lot better in the future."

The 43 points were the most allowed by the Ravens under Harbaugh and set a franchise-record for the most ever scored by the Texans (6-1).

Baltimore (5-2) was in its first game without future Hall of Fame middle linebacker Ray Lewis and top cornerback Lardarius Webb.

"We lost to a very good Houston Texans team," Baltimore outside linebacker Terrell Suggs said. "There's no sugarcoating it. Call a spade a spade."

The Ravens trailed 29-3 by halftime and were outscored 15-3 following Tandon Doss' touchdown catch during the early part of the third quarter.

Baltimore drove 45 yards for a Justin Tucker field goal on its first possession of the game, but was outgained 413-131 after that.

The Ravens were just 4-of-15 on third downs, something that was particularly frustrating to tight end Ed Dickson.

"Third downs," Dickson said. "You have to convert third downs."

There was a point during the second half Baltimore had twice as many drives that had ended in three-and-outs, turnovers or safeties (8) as it had first downs (4).

"Scoreboard. That tells it all," defensive end Pernell McPhee said. "43-13.

Quarterback Joe Flacco, who completed just 21 of his 43 passes for 147 yards during the loss to the Texans, passes during the fourth quarter. AP Images

That tells it all."

Flacco finished 21-of-43 for 147 yards with one touchdown and two interceptions. He had a quarterback rating of 45.4, one of the lowest marks of his career during the regular season.

He was sacked four times and had five passes batted down at the line of the scrimmage.

Houston outside linebacker Connor Barwin sacked Flacco for a safety with the Ravens leading 3-0 midway through the first quarter. Texans players referred to that play as a turning point in the game.

Prior to that, Houston's offense had picked up just one first down on its first three possessions.

"It's always one play that can ignite an offense, ignite a defense or ignite a team, period," Texans wide receiver Andre Johnson said. "I think that sack that Connor [Barwin] got for the safety was the play.... Once that happened, everything just fell in place."

The Texans' offense followed the safety with an 8-play, 67-yard drive that it capped with a 25-yard touchdown pass from quarterback Matt Schaub to wide receiver Kevin Walter.

Houston cornerback Johnathan Joseph intercepted Flacco on the first play of the Ravens' ensuing possession, returning it 52 yards for a score that pushed the Texans' lead to 16-3.

The pass was intended for wide receiver Torrey Smith, but was deflected by Texans defensive end J.J. Watt at the line of scrimmage and Joseph jumped in front of Smith to pull in the fluttering football.

Flacco targeted Smith and fellow starter Anquan Boldin 21 times, but the two combined for just seven catches.

No Baltimore pass catcher finished with more than 41 yards receiving.

"They ran their regular defense," Smith said of Houston. "I think the biggest thing of the game was batting down passes. They led to a few turnovers and stopped some drives."

Flacco had another tipped pass lead to an interception with the Ravens trailing 26-3 later in the second quarter after the offense had driven to Houston's 36-yard line.

Schaub followed by guiding a 12-play, 58-yard drive in the final minute of the half that ended with a 29-yard field goal from Shayne Graham.

Schaub was 23-of-37 for 256 yards and two touchdowns.

Johnson led the Texans with nine catches for 86 yards. Tight end Owen Daniels added seven catches for 59 yards and Walter hauled in four catches for 74 yards and the first quarter touchdown.

Houston also had 181 rushing yards, averaging nearly five yards per carry.

Arian Foster totaled 98 yards and two touchdowns on 19 carries.

Baltimore has given up 622 rushing yards in its last three games.

"It's frustrating because we didn't play great as a whole," Williams said. "Defense, offense didn't come to play today."

The Ravens have a bye next week before traveling to face the Cleveland Browns (1-6) Nov. 4.

"It's sad that we didn't get the job done, but we're going to right the ship during the break," Williams said. "Hopefully we can get things together." ■

Texans rookie linebacker Whitney Mercilus tips Joe Flacco's pass, leading to one of the Texans' two interceptions on the day. AP Images

Erie Victory

Ravens down Browns for "iffy" win

By Rich Dubroff

For half the game, the Baltimore Ravens offense could do no right.

The Ravens played a nearly perfect first quarter, then the offense stalled. Thanks to some stout defense and a key fourth-quarter drive, Baltimore escaped with a 25-15 win before 65,449 at Cleveland Browns Stadium on Sunday.

After their meltdown in Houston and a week off, the Ravens ran off a quick 14-0 lead after one quarter.

Baltimore (6-2) had 11 first downs in the first quarter, then nothing. It seemed like forever.

"The defense, they came over and motivated us to get to the next drive," Ray Rice said. "Terrell Suggs came over and said; 'We'll hold them from scoring touchdowns. You guys put a drive together, and let's win this game.'"

Both sides complied.

The Ravens defense never allowed the Browns (2-7) to get closer than the 11-yard line. Cleveland's Phil Dawson converted on five field goals, the last of which gave the Browns a 15-14 lead early in the fourth quarter.

"I was thinking that probably wasn't good," Baltimore coach John Harbaugh said. "I was thinking it would be nice to get a first down here."

After the fifth field goal, the Ravens put together their best drive since the first quarter, driving 81 yards to take a 22-14 lead on Joe Flacco's 19-yard pass to Torrey Smith and a two-point conversion to Anquan Boldin with 4:33 to play.

Harbaugh pointed to Flacco's 21-yard pass to Boldin that broke the 30-minute drought.

"The play to Anquan was the play," Harbaugh said.

That put the ball on Baltimore's 40-yard line. Cleveland's T.J. Ward was called for roughing the passer, giving the Ravens 15 crucial yards and Rice, who ran for 98 yards, but just 40 after the first quarter, had a 10-yard gain.

Two plays later, Flacco hit Smith, who dashed in for the score.

"It was all me," Smith said. "There were a few plays I felt like I could have made earlier in the game. I was frustrated by it, so I was glad we got to finish on the good side."

Flacco finished with 153 yards passing. In the last two games, he's been held to just 300. He converted on his first 10 passes, then missed eight of nine.

"It was tough to convert. They had it going, and we just didn't quite have it going at that point," Flacco said.

"I think that everybody does get

Running back Ray Rice carves out yardage during his 25-carry, 98-yard rushing performance against the Browns. AP Images

frustrated. It's just a matter of how you handle it. I think all of us were frustrated when we couldn't move the ball on third down."

Cleveland moved the ball smartly down the field, but then there seemed to be a crucial Ravens defensive play.

"Our job is to keep them out of the end zone. We made plays down there," Ed Reed said. "Us coming off a bye week, there might be a little rust. A couple of mistakes got made. We know we're fine-tuning things for the long haul."

"We've never been fancy. We've never been a pretty kind of team. I think the way we are winning games is just the way we continue to win," Rice said. "When you're 6-2, there's just no complaining about it."

This followed narrow wins against Kansas City and Dallas and the debacle in Houston. The Ravens are now 5-0 after the bye in the Harbaugh era.

Baltimore began quickly. Rice scored on an eight-yard run and Bernard Pierce had his first NFL touchdown with a second left in the quarter. The 14-0 lead made it look easy, but it was anything but.

Dawson hit field goals from 32, 28, 29, 33 and 41 yards to give the Browns their only lead.

"We have to play better than this," Ravens safety Bernard Pollard said. "We left some plays out there."

Cleveland's 29-year-old rookie quarterback Brandon Weeden had just 176 yards passing on 20-for-37. He threw two interceptions, one to Cary Williams, early in the third quarter, where the corner reversed direction and netted 29 artful yards and another to Reed in the closing moments.

"Our offense has done a great job. All we've got to do is play defense," Pollard said. "If we're sitting down for a little bit, we're going to be monstrous."

Harbaugh goes home happy because the team won, but not satisfied.

"We are going to try and become a great football team," he said. "We're not there by any stretch."

He'll remember the long two hours without a first down.

"We started fast and we ended well. In the middle, it was like this," Harbaugh said, waving his hand. "It was a little iffy." ■

Baltimore, Maryland • Ravens 55, Raiders 20

Record-Setting Win

Ravens score seven touchdowns, blow out Raiders
By Matt Zenitz

It all was an all-around demolition.

Joe Flacco threw three touchdowns, five different Ravens pass catchers had at least one catch of 25 yards or more and Baltimore even scored two touchdowns on special teams as it rolled to a 55-20 victory against a hapless Oakland Raiders team Sunday afternoon.

The 55 points established a new franchise-record for the Ravens and is the most scored by any team in the NFL this season.

Baltimore (7-2) maintains a narrow lead for first place in the AFC North ahead of the Pittsburgh Steelers (5-3).

Baltimore running back Ray Rice referred to the win against Oakland as "a confidence booster on all ends" heading into the Ravens' Nov. 18 showdown with the Steelers in Pittsburgh.

A week after going nearly two full quarters without gaining a single first down, and two weeks removed from being limited to 13 points in a blowout loss to the Houston Texans, the Ravens racked up 419 yards of total offense, the majority of which was accumulated during the first three quarters.

Baltimore led 10-0 by the end of the first quarter, extended its advantage to 27-10 by halftime and pushed its lead to 48-17 with five minutes still left in the third quarter.

"I thought we started fast, we finished well and we played pretty good in between, which we haven't always done," Ravens coach John Harbaugh said. "So, that's a good step in the right direction."

Flacco finished 21-of-33 for 341 yards with the three scoring passes and one interception. He completed five passes of 25 yards or longer, including three that went for gains of 40 yards or longer. He also had a 1-yard touchdown run on a quarterback sneak late in the first quarter.

Torrey Smith was the recipient of two of Flacco's three touchdown passes, including a 47-yarder to push Baltimore's lead to 34-10 just more than a minute into the third quarter.

Ed Dickson hauls in a first-half pass from Joe Flacco. The tight end had just two catches, but totaled 59 yards. DYLAN SLAGLE/STAFF PHOTO

Smith (two catches, 67 yards) was one of four Ravens pass catchers with 54 yards or more.

Tight ends Dennis Pitta (five catches, 67 yards, one touchdown) and Ed Dickson (two catches, 59 yards) combined for seven catches, 126 yards and a score. Jacoby Jones added 54 yards on two catches.

"I think the biggest thing was we executed well for the most part," Smith said. "We made a few mistakes here and there, but we came away with [a lot] of points and that's all you can really ask for."

The Raiders (3-6) limited the Ravens' ground game — Ray Rice had just 35 yards on 13 carries — but Flacco still managed to lead Baltimore to scores on eight of its first 10 possessions, including six touchdowns.

Oakland safety Tyvon Branch was asked after the game to grade the performance of the Raiders' pass defense.

Oakland entered Sunday ranked 21st in the NFL against the pass.

"Terrible," Branch said. "However you would grade that, we didn't play well today. We didn't play well enough to win. They put up a lot of points on us."

Raiders quarterback Carson Palmer threw for 368 yards and two scores, but he was limited aside from the two touchdown passes — a 55-yarder to Darrius Heyward-Bey and a 30-yarder to Denarius Moore. A good amount of his yards were picked up on screens and short passes to tight end Brandon Myers and fullback Marcel Reece.

Oakland was held without a touchdown on each of its first five possessions.

Without their top two running backs — Darren McFadden and Mike Goodson — the Raiders ran for just 72 yards on 24 carries.

McFadden and Goodson were both sidelined by high ankle sprains.

Baltimore recorded three sacks and forced three turnovers.

Outside linebacker Paul Kruger had six tackles, two sacks and an interception.

"I think a lot of guys are really starting to come around, and this defense is starting to gel together," Kruger said. "Things are kind of rolling our way. It's just a matter of us putting the right things together and trying to make plays. We did that today, and I think it's going to keep getting better."

The 35-point margin of victory was the largest for the Ravens since defeating the Detroit Lions, 48-3, on Dec. 13, 2009.

"This game is obviously something to build on and keep getting better," Baltimore left tackle Michael Oher said. "Obviously it's always good when you can score a lot of points, but it's something to build on.

"Having said that, I'm sure we are going to have a lot of corrections to make. Still, it's a great win." ∎

Opposite: Wide receiver Jacoby Jones, who caught three passes for 54 yards during the blowout victory, races past Raiders defensive back Michael Huff. Above: Kicker Justin Tucker had a busy day as the Ravens set a franchise record for points scored with 55. DYLAN SLAGLE/STAFF PHOTO

27

RUNNING BACK

Ray Rice

Fourth-down conversion against Chargers saved season

By Bob Blubaugh • February 1, 2013

It was the signature play of the Baltimore Ravens' 2012 regular season. The outlook was bleak. Trailing the Chargers by three points in San Diego on Nov. 25, the Ravens were facing a fourth-and-29 from their own 37-yard-line with less than two minutes to play.

"We needed a miracle," Ravens outside linebacker Terrell Suggs told reporters later.

It sure didn't look like they'd be getting one initially, when quarterback Joe Flacco dumped off a pass to Ray Rice just past the line of scrimmage.

"Check down, Hey Diddle Diddle, Ray Rice up the middle," Rice said after the game, uttering a catchphrase that soon turned up on T-shirts.

Then Rice did what he does in space.

He made two Chargers miss him with a nifty cut to the left near midfield. He shed a would-be tackler. He used his speed to outrun half the defense. Finally, he took advantage of an Anquan Boldin down-field block and bulled into two defenders to accumulate the required yardage.

The Ravens had done exactly what the Chargers had wanted them to do, thrown short in front of their entire defense. Yet Rice made it work for 31 yards and a first down.

"It's going to go down in history. It was just a remarkable play," Ravens coach John Harbaugh said afterward. "It was the greatest play I've ever seen or been a part of."

It was pretty important, too, given that it allowed the Ravens to kick a field goal to send the game into overtime, where they won it. Considering the Ravens finished with 10 wins — and it took 10 wins to reach the postseason — converting on fourth-and-29 played a major role in Baltimore's wild run to Super Bowl XLVII.

Rice had some big moments in the AFC playoffs, too.

In the Ravens' first playoff game, against Indianapolis, he took a screen pass in the right flat, made a gravity-defying spin move to elude a defender, and raced 47 yards just before halftime to set up the game's first touchdown and energize the offense.

In the AFC Championship game at New England, midway through the third quarter with the Ravens trailing by six points, virtually the same play again saw Rice make the initial defender miss and scamper 15 yards for a first down. Five plays later, Flacco threw a touchdown pass to put Baltimore ahead to stay.

In-between those two games, Rice carried 30 times for 131 yards and a touchdown in subfreezing conditions at Denver to help win that one.

Hard to imagine it, but five years ago, when

One of the NFL's most versatile running backs, Ray Rice acknowledges the fans at M&T Bank Stadium. DAVE MUNCH/STAFF PHOTO

he was a second-team All-American coming out of Rutgers, the knock on Rice was that he wasn't much of a pass-catcher out of the backfield (with only 37 receptions in three seasons) and that at 5-foot-8 and less than 200 pounds at the time, he wouldn't be durable enough to be an every-down back in the NFL.

Rice, who turned 26 on Jan. 22, disproved those theories long ago. Rice ran for 1,143 yards in 2012 — his fourth consecutive 1,000-yard season — and he has hauled in more than 300 receptions over that span.

After leading the league in yards from scrimmage in 2011, the ebullient back was rewarded with a five-year, $40-million contract that ensured the bulk of his career would be spent with the Ravens, Rice's goal all along after being taken by Baltimore in the second round of the 2008 draft.

"Hopefully, I'll retire a Raven," Rice said after signing the deal.

That'd be just fine with his many fans in the region. He has some 420,000 followers on Twitter and his jersey is perhaps the most visible on Sundays at M&T Bank Stadium and in workplaces on Purple Fridays around the state.

His backstory is well known.

Born in New Rochelle, N.Y., Rice had to begin dealing with adversity when his father was killed in a drive-by shooting when Rice was one year old. He and his three siblings were raised by his mother, a special education teacher. Rice endured more tragedy when a close cousin was killed by a drunk driver when Rice was in middle school.

Despite a standout high school career, Rice was just a three-star recruit and attended Rutgers, not exactly a football power when he went there. But he helped bring the program to prominence by rushing for a school record 4,926 yards in three seasons.

The Ravens liked him even before they picked him.

"He makes things happen in space," then-college scouting director Eric DeCosta said before the 2008 draft.

While the Ravens didn't receive overwhelming marks for their haul of quarterback Joe Flacco in the first round and Rice in the second — *USA Today,* CBS Sports and the *Washington Post* gave Baltimore only a "C" grade for its draft performance — the Ravens were impressed by Rice the moment he stepped onto their Owings Mills practice field.

"I just think he's our kind of guy," Harbaugh said after Rice's first minicamp. "That's high character, he's tough, rough, loves to play football.... He's from a great family, and he's not just a one-play playmaker. He's a durable playmaker."

Added Willis McGahee, the team's feature back at the time: "That kid can flat-out play. Man, he's quick."

Rice spent just one year as McGahee's understudy, giving a glimpse of what was to come with a 156-yard rushing performance against Cleveland in Week 9 when McGahee was injured.

In 2009, Rice averaged 5.3 yards per carry and made the Pro Bowl in his first season as a starter. He went 83 yards for a touchdown on the Ravens' first play from scrimmage in their playoff win at New England that season.

He showed his durability by rushing a career-high 307 times in 2010, then set a career mark with 1,364 rushing yards in 2011.

This marked his fourth consecutive season of at least 60 receptions. While he has rushed for more than 5,000 yards — second to Jamal Lewis in Ravens history — he knows it is his ability to catch passes, and make something happen, that sets him apart.

"If you are a running back and you are not able to catch, then you become one-dimensional.... I think the catching was what really put it over the top for me," Rice said last summer.

His numbers were down a bit this season. His

Running back Ray Rice, who rushed for 1,143 yards and nine touchdowns during the 2012 season, stretches before a July 26 practice. DYLAN SLAGLE/STAFF PHOTO

1,143 rushing yards and 61 receptions were his lowest totals since his rookie year. The Ravens began using bigger back Bernard Pierce to spell Rice more and more over the latter portion of the regular season.

None of the numbers matters nearly as much as winning to Rice.

"Stats and all the other good stuff, you could throw all that aside, because one thing about our group ... we are very unselfish," he said. "It doesn't matter who is getting the job done as long as we are getting the job done when we go out and execute."

The always-smiling Rice could barely contain himself in the days before the team left for New Orleans.

"I'm not going to shy around and say this isn't the best feeling of my life," Rice said. "I have been down to a few Super Bowl appearances, but I told myself I'm never going to one unless I'm playing it. This is the one that I finally get to say 'I'm playing in it.'"

And Rice's spectacular catch-and-run on Nov. 25 in San Diego is as big a reason as any why he and the Ravens have a chance to raise the Lombardi Trophy.

"You won't see too many plays like that," Ravens receiver Torrey Smith told reporters that day. "He was the perfect guy for it." ■

REGULAR SEASON • NOVEMBER 18, 2012

Pittsburgh, Pennsylvania • Ravens 13, Steelers 10

Stronger Than Steel

No offense, no problem for Ravens

By Matt Zenitz

The Ravens' offense could seemingly do no right.

Joe Flacco struggled against the Steelers' top-ranked pass defense, Ray Rice was held in check by Pittsburgh's rush defense and Baltimore was held without a single offensive touchdown.

But the Ravens got a touchdown return from Jacoby Jones for the second straight week, kept the Steelers out of the end zone following an early first quarter score and managed to pull out an important 13-10 victory against rival Pittsburgh Sunday night at Heinz Field.

"Whatever procedure my brother had, I think I'm going to need. My heart's beating a little fast right now," Baltimore head coach John Harbaugh joked after the game, referencing a minor heart procedure his brother, Jim, had earlier in the week.

With the win, Baltimore (8-2) takes a two-game lead on the Steelers (6-4) for first place in the AFC North.

The Ravens were outgained 311-200, held to their lowest offensive output of the season, but never relinquished the lead following Jones' 63-yard punt return for a touchdown that staked them a 10-7 advantage midway through the first quarter.

Baltimore picked up just 12 first downs, including only four in the second half, Flacco finished with just 164 yards passing, Rice was limited to 40 yards on 20 carries and the Ravens were held to just 64 yards of total offense in the second half. Yet, it proved to be enough as Pittsburgh's offense sputtered without injured quarterback Ben Roethlisberger.

His replacement, Byron Leftwich, capped the Steelers' opening possession with a 31-yard touchdown run, but he finished just 17-of-38 for 201 yards with an interception and no touchdown passes.

He had the Steelers driving for a potential game-tying or go-ahead score midway the fourth quarter, but was sacked on a third-and-11 after Pittsburgh had worked the ball to Baltimore's 43-yard line.

The Steelers were forced to punt with 4:21 left in the quarter and the

Cornerback Corey Graham, who played a key role in the Ravens' injury-plagued secondary, bats a touchdown pass intended for Steelers wide receiver Jerricho Cotchery. AP Images

Ravens' offense followed by picking up two first downs. Pittsburgh's offense eventually got the ball back at its own 16-yard line with just more than a minute remaining, but it picked up just 12 yards before being forced to resort to laterals on the last play of the game, an unsuccessful sequence that ended with a fumble recovery by Baltimore linebacker Courtney Upshaw.

"This was just a great win," Harbaugh said. "Congratulations to Pittsburgh. They played their hearts out, like they always do. And congratulations to our team. They played their hearts out, like they always do, finding a way to win a very tough football game the way we did."

Sunday marked the ninth time in the last 11 meetings between the Ravens and Steelers that the game was decided by a touchdown or less.

"It's never pretty in this game," Harbaugh said. "I think it's the usual, the three-point spread. Isn't that what these usually are? So we got a typical Pittsburgh-Baltimore game.

"That was a great defensive struggle, which is not unusual."

And while the Ravens were held without an offensive touchdown, their defense forced either a turnover or a punt on 11 of Pittsburgh's final 12 possessions.

"As the game went on, I think after that first drive, we stepped it up and got a great defensive performance the rest of the game outside of the first drive," Baltimore defensive tackle Haloti Ngata said.

With the win, the Ravens improve to 8-2 for the first time under Harbaugh and for just the second time in franchise history.

Baltimore is one of just six teams in the AFC with a winning record. The Texans (9-1) are the only team in the conference with a better record than Baltimore.

"I'm happy right now," Jones said. "8-2, can't complain." ■

Jacoby Jones returns a first-quarter punt 63 yards for Baltimore's lone touchdown during its win over the Steelers in Pittsburgh. AP Images

REGULAR SEASON • NOVEMBER 25, 2012

San Diego, California • Ravens 16, Chargers 13 (OT)

"Remarkable" Play Saves Game

Rice converts on fourth-and-29 to keep hope alive, Tucker wins it in OT

By Matt Zenitz

The game looked to be lost.

Down by three. Less than two minutes remaining in the fourth quarter. Fourth down with 29 yards needed to convert a first down.

Anything less than 29 yards and game over.

And, really, the outlook looked even less promising when Ray Rice hauled in Joe Flacco's fourth-down pass just three yards beyond the line of scrimmage with eight members of the San Diego Chargers defense in front of him and 26 additional yards needed to convert a game-extending first down.

The end result? A play that Ravens wide receiver Torrey Smith joked afterward that he couldn't even replicate in a video game.

Rice ran for 10 yards down the right sideline, cut back toward the opposite sideline when three Chargers defenders converged near midfield, picked up a key block from wide receiver Anquan Boldin 10 yards later and eventually lowered his shoulder into two San Diego defenders, pushing forward to the 34-yard line for the finishing touches of a 29-yard gain and an improbable first down converting catch-and-run.

Justin Tucker kicked a game-tying 38-yard field goal six plays later as time expired in regulation. And after Flacco engineered a 69-yard drive on the Ravens' second possession of overtime, Tucker booted another 38-yard field goal, this one lifting Baltimore to an implausible 16-13 victory Sunday at San Diego's Qualcomm Stadium — a win that wouldn't have been possible without Rice's fourth quarter heroics.

Running back Ray Rice converts a fourth-and-29, a season-saving play, which led to the game-tying field goal against the Chargers. AP Images

"We're all going to talk about the fourth-and-29 play," Ravens head coach John Harbaugh said. "It's going to go down in history. It was just a remarkable play.... It was the greatest play I've ever seen or been a part of. It was 11 guys who made the play happen, but one guy had a real big role in it. It was a sensational play by Ray Rice."

A sensational play that produced the longest fourth down conversion in more than a decade — the longest since the Buffalo Bills converted a fourth-and-34 in 2001.

"It was just total will," Rice told reporters after the game. "Once I made the first guy miss when I cut back across the grain, I actually saw the defense had to flip their hip and I kept eyeing the first down. I looked and [thought], 'Should I keep running to the sideline or should I just keep trying to get up field?' And that's what I did. I just kept getting up field.... I'm just glad we came out on top."

Added Smith: "I had a great view.... That's probably one of the best plays I've ever seen. You won't see too many plays like that. He was the perfect guy for it."

But the Ravens still needed some late heroics from their defense and Flacco as well.

And after the defense forced a three-and-out on San Diego's second possession of overtime, Flacco led a 12-play, 69-yard drive to put Baltimore in position for Tucker's game-winning field goal.

Said Harbaugh: "To see it come together in a victory like that, on the road, against a very good team — that's what it's all about."

The Ravens trailed 10-0 at halftime and 13-3 midway through the fourth quarter, but Flacco threw a 4-yard touchdown to Dennis Pitta with just more than four minutes remaining. Baltimore's defense forced a three-and-out on San Diego's next possession, setting the stage for the offense's game-tying drive highlighted by Rice's fourth-and-29 conversion.

Flacco was 18-of-27 for 222 yards with a touchdown during the fourth quarter and overtime after throwing for just 131 yards during the first three quarters while completing only 12 of his first 27 pass attempts.

"Obviously we were forced to open it up a little bit," Harbaugh told reporters in San Diego. "Joe completed a couple passes, and he just got into a little bit of a rhythm.

"When Joe can get into a little bit of a rhythm ... he's difficult to deal with, and he was able to get started. It took longer than we'd hoped, but it was just in time."

Smith finished with a career-high seven catches for a season-best 144 yards, including the acrobatic 31-yard grab in overtime to set up Tucker's game-winning field goal.

Smith also had a 54-yard catch-and-run early in the third quarter to put Baltimore in position for a 43-yard Tucker field goal after the team had been held scoreless on each of its six first half possessions.

"Torrey is getting to the point where he can pretty much run all those routes really effectively," Harbaugh said. "So, that's a credit to him, and it's really a big weapon for us."

The Ravens' defense, meanwhile, held a potent Chargers offense scoreless on six of their final seven possessions.

A year after yielding 415 yards to San Diego amid a 34-14 defeat, Baltimore limited the Chargers to just 280 yards in four-plus quarters of action.

With the win — and a Pittsburgh Steelers loss to the Cleveland Browns — the Ravens now lead the AFC North by three games with just five games remaining in the regular season.

"The thing the guys have done as a team.... Our guys have positioned themselves very well," Harbaugh said. "To take advantage of an opportunity, that's what you try to do. We talked. Every game you win, it makes that next game that much more important." ■

Receiver Anquan Bolden elevates to make one of his two receptions during the Ravens' overtime victory in San Diego. AP Images

55
LINEBACKER

Terrell Suggs

Star recovers on the job from Achilles injury
By Matt Zenitz • January 27, 2013

It was obvious to his coaches. It was obvious to his teammates. It was obvious to the media that covers the team. And it was even obvious to the casual fan. Baltimore Ravens outside linebacker Terrell Suggs simply wasn't the same player from a physical standpoint.

His speed and quickness were diminished. He wasn't in optimal playing shape after missing all of the offseason, all of the preseason and the beginning part of the regular season. And he just wasn't the same imposing, dominant physical presence that he was during his NFL Defensive Player of the Year season just a year earlier.

Not like it should've been a surprise, though.

Suggs returned to action in mid-October just more than five months after suffering a tear of his right Achilles that most assumed at the time would sideline him for the entire 2012 season.

But it didn't. And for as much as he struggled at times while working back from the injury, and for as much as he may have appeared limited during the regular season, it's been a different Suggs on display during the playoffs.

He's gotten progressively more comfortable with the surgically-repaired Achilles tendon. He's noticeably quicker and more explosive than he was in mid-October. And, to Ravens coach John Harbaugh, Suggs is starting to look more like the dominating player that he was prior to sustaining the injury.

"He's getting better," Harbaugh said. "He's becoming quicker, faster, more explosive — all of those things. You can tell that [the Achilles] is healing. He's just playing more like a normal 100-percent Terrell Suggs would play."

Suggs suffered the torn Achilles tendon in early May, an injury that typically takes six to eight months to recover from. But Suggs was back on the practice field Oct. 17 and started against the Houston Texans just five days later.

And even with Suggs' production having been limited in the weeks leading up to Baltimore's wild-card game against the Indianapolis Colts as he continued to work back from the Achilles injury — while also playing through a torn right biceps he suffered in early December — Ravens

After hitting Colts quarterback Andrew Luck during the Ravens' playoff win, linebacker Terrell Suggs provides some words of wisdom to the rookie. DYLAN SLAGLE/STAFF PHOTO

defensive coordinator Dean Pees said at the time that he still "marveled" that Suggs was even on the field at all.

"The fact that this guy came back from an Achilles [injury] in and of itself ... I don't know about you guys, but I am marveled the guy has played at all this year," Pees said in early January. "So I think anything that we've gotten out of Terrell Suggs has been a positive.

"I don't look at it at all like he hasn't done something successfully. I look at it as this has been a bonus that we ever had the guy. I never dreamed that we'd ever have the guy at all this year, so anything we've gotten out of him, to me, is a positive and a bonus."

But for as restricted as Suggs may have been by the injuries during the regular season, and for as much as his production may have been down as a result, it's been a different, much healthier looking and much more impactful Suggs throughout the playoffs.

He's been a strong edge-setter in the run game. He's been active in run pursuit. And he's been a difference-maker as a pass rusher.

"It's crazy," Ravens defensive end Pernell McPhee said. "You could look at [Suggs] when he first came back and be like, 'Oh yeah, he's not the same Suggs.' But then, as the season kept going, he kept getting better at things and better at his technique. And then the playoffs hit and he just got explosive.

"The playoffs hit, you could turn on the tape and he was real explosive. He's been explosive all playoffs, all three playoff games. That's the exciting part."

And after tallying just 22 tackles and two sacks during the regular season, Suggs has 19 tackles, two sacks and a forced fumble in the playoffs.

He had 10 tackles, two sacks and a forced fumble during Baltimore's divisional round win over Peyton Manning and the Denver Broncos and then seven tackles in the Ravens' AFC championship victory over Tom Brady and the New England Patriots.

"You can just see he's playing a lot more freely, and he's not really stressing about things as much," fellow outside linebacker Albert McClellan said of Suggs. "He's shining.... He's been huge. And he demands a double-team, or he demands attention, which is letting other people come free and just opening up a lot of things for everybody else."

Added defensive end Arthur Jones: "Yeah, he's absolutely getting healthier, and a healthy Terrell Suggs is an animal.... You can tell he's feeling a lot more comfortable with his injuries." And, according to McPhee, that's something that's continued to show during the Ravens' preparation for Super Bowl XLVII.

"He's got a lot of confidence," McPhee said of Suggs. "He feels like he's got a lot of his speed back. I [saw] him working some moves the other day in practice ... that I hadn't seen him do all year.... I'm ready for him to go out there and shine on Super Bowl Sunday." ■

Linebacker Terrell Suggs helps a host of Ravens gang tackle Steelers running back Isaac Redman during a 23-20 Baltimore loss. DYLAN SLAGLE/STAFF PHOTO

REGULAR SEASON • DECEMBER 2, 2012

Baltimore, Maryland • Steelers 23, Ravens 20

Offensive Performance

Passing game falters as Ravens fall to Steelers

By Matt Zenitz

Joe Flacco's pass seemingly never had a chance.

Tight end Dennis Pitta was surrounded by three Pittsburgh Steelers defenders as he turned up the right sideline, yet Flacco decided to float a pass in his direction anyway, an ill-advised attempt that was easily intercepted by Pittsburgh safety Ryan Clark.

It was that kind of night for Flacco and the Baltimore Ravens' passing game.

Off-target, out of rhythm and plagued by poor decision-making for much of Sunday's 23-20 loss to the Steelers, Flacco finished just 16-of-34 for 188 yards with one touchdown and two turnovers, including the second quarter interception.

His fumble midway through the fourth quarter led to a Steelers game-tying touchdown. And after Flacco and the offense stalled on Baltimore's ensuing possession, Steelers third-string quarterback Charlie Batch, starting in place of injured starter Ben Roethlisberger, guided a game-winning scoring drive that ended with Shaun Suisham's 42-yard field goal as time expired.

"We don't feel good right now, obviously," Flacco said after the game, later adding, "I felt like we could have moved the ball today, and we didn't do what we needed to do to have that happen today."

The Ravens led 13-6 at halftime, but picked up just 97 yards in the second half.

Four of Baltimore's final five possessions ended in either a punt or a turnover.

"We've just got to make plays," Ravens wide receiver Torrey Smith said. "It's that simple. They didn't do anything special. We've just got to make plays."

Pittsburgh's offense wasn't perfect either with its third-string quarterback under center, but came to life in the second half.

Batch was limited to just 57 yards through the air in the first half, but led three second half scoring drives, including the two in the fourth quarter.

He finished 25-of-36 for 276 yards with one touchdown and one interception.

Steelers linebacker Larry Foote sacks quarterback Joe Flacco. The Ravens allowed three sacks during the 23-20 loss. DYLAN SLAGLE/STAFF PHOTO

Batch was making just his ninth start since 2002 and his yardage represented his largest output since 2001.

Batch was 16-of-20 for 219 yards with both the touchdown and the interception in the second half.

He completed five passes of 17 yards or longer during the second half, including a 43-yarder to tight end Heath Miller early in the third quarter that set up a Jonathan Dwyer 16-yard touchdown run.

The Steelers outgained the Ravens 273-97 in the second half and picked up 14 of their 19 first downs after halftime.

"They made plays," Ravens safety Ed Reed said. "They made adjustments to certain things we were running. They made the plays, and we just have to play with better, better composure and be smarter with the ball. You can't turn the ball over [on offense] and you have to get off the field on third down [on defense]. I don't think we did either one."

Batch connected with Miller for a 7-yard touchdown to tie the score at 20 midway through the fourth quarter just four plays after Flacco's fumble gave the Steelers' offense possession at Baltimore's 27-yard line.

Flacco connected with fullback Vonta Leach for a 12-yard gain on the Ravens' next play from scrimmage, but followed with three straight incompletions.

Sam Koch's punt pinned the Steelers at their own 15-yard line, but Batch guided a 12-play, 61-yard drive that ended with Suisham's game-winning field goal as time expired.

"It was a very emotional game, a very disappointing loss, a very tough loss" Baltimore coach John Harbaugh said. "Compliments to Pittsburgh coming in. They played very well. They did a nice job in the turnover battle, obviously, and won the game. I'm very disappointed. There are a lot of things we could have done better." ■

Steelers linebacker Jason Worilds forces Ravens fullback Vonta Leach out of bounds. Leach caught four passes during the loss. DYLAN SLAGLE/ STAFF PHOTO

REGULAR SEASON • DECEMBER 9, 2012

Landover, Maryland • Redskins 31, Ravens 28 (OT)

"Rough Loss" For Ravens

Redskins rally late, win on overtime kick

By Matt Zenitz

Ray Rice barreled through a gaping hole on the left side of the line, crossing the goal line untouched before stopping for a brief moment to playfully flex his left arm at the opposing crowd.

The game appeared to be in hand.

The crowd had quieted, the Ravens led by eight with less than five minutes left in the fourth quarter and the Redskins needed a touchdown and a two-point conversion against a Baltimore defense that had stiffened after some early struggles.

But, for the second straight week, the Ravens' defense couldn't come up with a decisive stop late.

Washington backup quarterback Kirk Cousins tossed a late touchdown pass and scored a game-tying two-point conversion moments later to force overtime.

And after Baltimore's offense went three-and-out on the first possession of the extra period, Redskins return specialist Richard Crawford broke a 64-yard punt return to set up Kai Fortbath's game-winning 34-yard field goal to lift Washington to a 31-28 victory against the Ravens Sunday afternoon.

"It was a hard, tough and disappointing loss," Baltimore coach John Harbaugh said.

The Ravens led for the majority of the second half, pushing their lead to 28-20 on Rice's 7-yard scoring run with four minutes, 47 seconds left in the fourth quarter. But Robert Griffin III battled through a sprained knee to lead the Redskins into scoring position on their ensuing possession, a drive capped by Cousins' 11-yard scoring pass to Pierre Garcon with 36 seconds remaining.

Cousins ran in for a game-tying two-point conversion moments later.

Cousins replaced the injured Griffin after Griffin had guided Washington to Baltimore's 16-yard line.

In overtime, the Redskins forced a three-and-out on the Ravens' opening possession of the extra period, Crawford returned Sam Koch's punt 64 yards to Baltimore's 24-yard line and Forbath

Rookie running back Bernard Pierce, whose rugged style adeptly complements that of veteran starter Ray Rice, vaults over Redskins cornerback DeAngelo Hall. AP Images

drilled his game-winning field goal just three plays later.

"It's always tough, especially when you think you have the game won," Rice said.

Forbath's kick lifted Washington (7-6) to its fourth straight win and sent Baltimore (9-4) to its second straight defeat on a field goal as time expired.

Just a week earlier, the Ravens blew a 20-13 fourth quarter lead on the Steelers, eventually falling 23-20 on a Shaun Suisham field goal as time ran out.

"It's frustrating," Baltimore wide receiver Torrey Smith. "It's frustrating, especially that it's played out [like that] two weeks in a row. To lose like this, it's very frustrating."

The Ravens had plenty of chances to avoid it.

Each of their five second-half possessions stretched to at least their own 44-yard line — with three advancing into Redskins territory — but the five drives resulted in two turnovers, two punts and just one touchdown.

Flacco finished 16-of-21 for 189 yards with three touchdowns, but had two turnovers during the second half — one fumble and one interception.

His fumble, which came on Baltimore's opening possession of the half, helped set up a Forbath 48-yard field goal that trimmed Washington's deficit to 21-17.

Flacco tossed an interception on the Ravens' ensuing drive with Baltimore facing a third-and-six from the Redskins' 11-yard line.

"The second half, it was probably just turnovers," Flacco said. "We did a good job running the ball. The one probably down in our zone [the fumble] is probably the one that hurt the most on my part. Other than that, I don't think we did too bad of a job.

"We were able to grind some drives. We moved the ball pretty decently, [but] we just weren't able to finish. We had penalties that hurt us early on. We kind of stopped ourselves today more than we did get stopped."

The Ravens finished with 359 yards of total offense and picked up 18 first downs. Flacco had the three scoring passes while Rice and Bernard Pierce combined to rush for 174 yards against the NFL's fourth-ranked rush defense.

But after scoring touchdowns on three of its first four possessions, and building a 21-14 second quarter lead, Baltimore's offense was held without a score on each of its next five drives prior to the fourth quarter march that ended in Rice's 7-yard scoring run.

"We were moving the ball. We just didn't finish," Smith said.

And the Ravens' defense couldn't come up with the stop late.

The group yielded two early touchdowns as Washington jumped out to an early 14-7 lead, but tightened up from there until the Redskins' final drive of regulation when Griffin and Cousins combined to guide Washington 85 yards in 13 plays for the game-tying score.

"They made some plays, made a play, and hats off to them," Ravens safety Ed Reed said. "They played a great game. We played a great game, but just too many mistakes." ▪

Defensive end Arthur Jones tackles elusive Redskins quarterback Robert Griffin III during the loss to Washington, Baltimore's cross-town rival. AP Images

Ravens Can Cameron

Erratic unit ranked only 18th in total offense; Caldwell named OC

By Matt Zenitz • December 11, 2012

Just three months ago the Ravens looked to be on the brink of a breakthrough season offensively. There was excitement from players and coaches surrounding the team's new no-huddle offense, substantial optimism regarding the development of quarterback Joe Flacco and genuine enthusiasm about what appeared to be the deepest and most talented group of skill position players in team history.

This was supposed to be the year that the Ravens took that proverbial next step as an offense, establishing themselves as one of the league's truly elite groups.

Instead, Baltimore's offense has been wildly erratic, as has Flacco, and offensive coordinator Cam Cameron, as had been the case in previous seasons as well, was criticized for his incorporation, or lack thereof, of running back Ray Rice into the team's offense.

And just three months after the Ravens scored 44 points in a season-opening blowout of the Bengals, Cameron was fired Monday after nearly five years as Baltimore's offensive coordinator. He'll be replaced by quarterbacks coach Jim Caldwell.

"It's just an opportunity to get this going and become the offense and the best team that we can be, and we feel like it's what's best for the team at this time," Ravens head coach John Harbaugh said. "That's why we made the move."

Baltimore is ranked ninth in the league in scoring, but is just 18th out of the league's 32 teams in total offense. Flacco, meanwhile, has regressed after an impressive start to the season. He's been limited to 188 yards or less in six of the Ravens' last nine games and his total quarterback rating (total QBR), as generated by ESPN, is just 21st out of NFL quarterbacks. At the same time, Rice, widely regarded as Baltimore's best offensive weapon, has seen a surprisingly limited workload at times.

Cameron's firing comes just a day after the Ravens' 31-28 overtime loss to the Redskins, a game during which the Ravens scored touchdowns on three of their first four possessions before going scoreless on their first five drives of the second half.

Harbaugh, however, said his decision to part ways with Cameron wasn't based off anything "specific" that happened Sunday.

"Not specific," Harbaugh said. "I mean, we

put 28 points up, so you're not going to say it was a reaction to a down offensive performance. It's not that, and I think that's really important to point out. It would be really easy to go the route that says it's a result of something and somebody's taking the blame for something. It's not that.

"People are going to believe what they're going to believe. It's what I believe is best going forward for our offense and our football team. That's not to say anybody can't do the job, or didn't do the job. Cam was doing a heck of a job ... but I also believe right now, at this time, the timing says this is the best thing, and that's what we're going to do."

Baltimore did show glimpses of being a high-powered offense under Cameron — the Ravens tallied 30 points or more 26 times during Cameron's almost five seasons as offensive coordinator — but, overall, Cameron's offense was consistently inconsistent.

The Ravens were among the bottom half of the NFL in total offense during three of Cameron's five seasons with the team and never finished a season ranked better than 13th in the category.

Nonetheless, the timing of Cameron's dismissal was surprising.

Despite its offensive struggles, and any issues it's had defensively, Baltimore is 9-4 and leads the AFC North by two games with just three games left in the regular season.

Harbaugh said he didn't feel like the timing of the move would be disruptive to the team.

"That's always a consideration," Harbaugh said. "That's one of things you think about, and there are a lot of considerations. You try to take all of that into account and try to come to a conclusion about what is best for your football team.... Every decision is based on what's best for the team.

"I don't think it will be disruptive. I think it will be positive. I believe that, but it will be up to all of us to make it that way."

Harbaugh declined to say who else had input in the decision, and said that Flacco wasn't consulted,

DYLAN SLAGLE/STAFF PHOTO

instead emphasizing: "The decision was mine."

"This is an opportunity for us to try and win some football games, and to try and be the best football team we can be," Harbaugh said.

Caldwell was hired by the Ravens in January after 10 seasons with the Colts — the final three of which he served as the team's head coach.

Caldwell has never served as offensive coordinator before, but is a respected offensive mind that is credited for playing a primary role in the development of quarterback Peyton Manning.

"Jim is qualified," Harbaugh said. "Jim's a heck of a coach, and we've got a heck of a staff. He'll do a great job. I'm looking forward to seeing how it plays out." ■

REGULAR SEASON • DECEMBER 16, 2012
Baltimore, Maryland • Broncos 34, Ravens 17

Skid Hits Three

Offense fails as streaking Broncos top Ravens

By Matt Zenitz

Elvis Dumervil eluded the block of Ravens left tackle Michael Oher, easily working his way into Baltimore's backfield to throw Joe Flacco for a sack and provide one final bit of frustration for the Ravens' offense.

The sack provided a fitting end for Baltimore's offense amid Sunday's 34-17 loss to the Broncos.

Cam Cameron may be gone, but many of the issues that plagued the offense prior to Cameron's dismissal remain.

The Ravens' first seven possessions Sunday consisted of five three-and-outs and two turnovers, and they didn't score their first touchdown until already trailing 31-3 early in the fourth quarter.

"I think it was a matter of us going out there and not doing some of the simple things right early on," Flacco said, "and it kind of took us awhile to get into that groove that we really needed to be successful."

But, as was the case even prior to Sunday, the offensive struggles were about more than just the offensive coordinator.

Flacco was erratic, the offensive line struggled at times — both in pass protection as well as in the run game — and the Ravens' receiving corps had problems getting open against a physical and athletic Broncos secondary.

"We just, as players, didn't execute as cleanly as we would have liked," Baltimore tight end Dennis Pitta said. "There's a lot of plays out there we would like to have back."

None more so than Flacco's interception in the final minute of the second quarter.

With the Ravens trailing just 10-0 and facing a first-and-goal from Denver's 4-yard line, Flacco was intercepted by Broncos safety Chris Harris. Harris returned the interception 98 yards for a momentum-shifting touchdown.

"As much as we weren't playing very well in the first half, we still had that opportunity at the end of it to go down there, put points on the board and really put a

Broncos defensive end Elvis Dumervil sacks quarterback Joe Flacco during the fourth quarter of the Ravens' 34-17 loss. DYLAN SLAGLE/STAFF PHOTO

two touchdown returns from Trindon Holliday.

Flacco averaged more than 18 yards per completion against a Denver pass defense that ranked as the NFL's third-best during the regular season.

"Joe makes big plays when we have to have them, and he stays poised all throughout," Pitta said. "He was unbelievable this game."

It was the continuation of an impressive past month for Flacco, a quarterback that tight end Ed Dickson said earlier in the week is "hitting his peak" right now.

Saturday was Flacco's fifth game with Jim Caldwell as offensive coordinator. Flacco struggled in his first game under Caldwell — the Dec. 16 loss to Denver — but he's flourished since.

He played only sparingly in the Ravens' regular season finale, but he's thrown for 922 yards and seven touchdowns without an interception in the other three games since that loss to the Broncos.

Cam Cameron was the Ravens' offensive coordinator for Flacco's first four-plus NFL seasons before being fired in early December.

And after being limited to 188 yards or less in six of his final nine games under Cameron, Flacco's thrown for 282 yards or more in the last three games that he's seen a full workload under Caldwell.

"Joe's really been throwing it well," Pitta said earlier in the week. "We've had confidence in him all year, but I think with the regime change — and with Jim calling the plays — I think that things have been a little different and Joe's really comfortable in the things that we're doing now and really able to kind of get more in a rhythm during games, so that's certainly helped him out."

And that continued to be the case Saturday.

"Joe Flacco's been playing lights out," Baltimore running back Ray Rice said. "He will lead us to the Super Bowl. Our offense goes through Joe. So when Joe plays at a high level like that, it makes everything a lot smoother." ■

Quarterback Joe Flacco readies to throw during Baltimore's 13-10 win against the rival Steelers.
AP Images

Baltimore, Maryland • Ravens 24, Colts 9

Lewis Returns, Leads Ravens

Flacco rebounds from slow start, offense comes to life

By Matt Zenitz

Three errant Joe Flacco passes that were nearly intercepted. Three drops by Ravens receivers, including two on would-be touchdowns. And just four completions for Flacco on his first 11 pass attempts.

It wasn't exactly an encouraging start for Flacco and Baltimore's passing game amid Sunday's AFC Wild Card matchup with the Indianapolis Colts.

But Flacco and the passing game came to life in the second half.

And behind two second half Flacco scoring passes, the Ravens cruised to a 24-9 victory against the Colts in sending future Hall of Fame linebacker Ray Lewis out with a win in the final home game of his storied career while also setting the stage for a divisional round showdown with the Denver Broncos Saturday in Denver.

"For us, we came out during the week and we wanted to show them a couple looks and see what we got early," Baltimore wide

receiver Anquan Boldin said. "We kind of wanted to hold some things back until the second half.... They played some things a little different than what we expected the first half. The second half, we made adjustments and came out and opened it up a little bit."

And despite the slow start, Flacco finished with 282 yards and two touchdowns. He had 174 yards and both scoring passes in the second half, including a 20-yarder to tight end Dennis Pitta that pushed the Ravens' lead to 17-6 midway through the third quarter. He added an 18-yard scoring pass to Boldin midway through the fourth quarter.

Flacco completed eight of his final 11 pass attempts after the 4-for-11 start and had eight passes that went for gains of 18 yards or longer.

"Joe made some tremendous throws," Baltimore head coach John Harbaugh

Ray Rice rumbles past linebacker Robert Mathis and other Colts defenders during Baltimore's 24-9 victory. DYLAN SLAGLE/STAFF PHOTO

said. "He made some throws under pressure, with two guys coming off the edge. He got hit a couple times, but he made the throws. I thought Joe threw the ball down field incredibly well.... He played at a really high level."

As did Boldin.

The physical veteran receiver was held without a catch in the first half, but he finished with five grabs for a Ravens playoff record 145 yards and the touchdown.

"He went over the top. He went underneath. He just did what he's been doing all year long, and we just went to him," Baltimore fullback Vonta Leach said of Boldin.

Boldin had four catches that produced gains of 18 yards or more, including a 46-yard grab midway through the third quarter that helped set up Flacco's scoring pass to Pitta.

"Anquan always comes up big for us," Ravens tight end Ed Dickson said. "He's one of our leaders on offense and we follow his lead. For the most part, I thought we played a pretty good game all-around on offense. We just have a couple things that we need to clean up and get ready for next week."

Baltimore finished with 441 yards of total offense and 18 first downs.

Ray Rice had two fumbles, but he combined with rookie Bernard Pierce for 220 yards from scrimmage.

Pierce totaled 103 yards on 13 carries. Rice posted 70 yards on 15 carries and had a 47-yard catch-and-run late in the second quarter to set up a 2-yard Leach scoring run that helped the Ravens head into the half with a 10-6 lead.

"I think we did what we had to do to come out with this win," Leach said. "We put some points on the board. Anquan Boldin was huge for us today. So was the running game, which got going a little bit and opened up everything else. I mean, hey, when

Terrell Suggs, Haloti Ngata and Pernell McPhee combine for one of the defense's three sacks of Colts rookie quarterback Andrew Luck. DYLAN SLAGLE/STAFF PHOTO

we go down the field and we're hitting on all cylinders like that it's going to be hard to beat us."

Indianapolis had success moving the ball as well — accumulating 419 yards and 25 first downs – but was limited to just three Adam Vinatieri field goals.

The Colts were held scoreless on four of their five second half possessions despite four of the five drives stretching into Baltimore territory.

Indianapolis rookie quarterback Andrew Luck threw for 288 yards, but he completed just 28 of his 54 pass attempts and tossed a key interception a little more than midway through the fourth quarter with Indianapolis trailing 24-9 and facing a fourth-and-1 at the Ravens' 18-yard line.

"We had some miscues.... But, in the red zone, we stepped it up, which was huge," Baltimore safety Ed Reed said. "We kept them out of the end zone."

Lewis contributed with a team-high 13 tackles. He was playing in his first game since suffering a torn right triceps in mid-October.

The 37-year old announced Wednesday that he plans to retire following the conclusion of the season, meaning Sunday was his final time playing inside M&T Bank Stadium.

"That probably won't sink in [yet]," Lewis said. "You know what, the reason why it probably won't is because it's probably the last thing on my mind right now. Seriously, because the next thing on my mind is, as a team, we are poised to go do something. ... We made a commitment to each other, and that is to next week head to Denver to get a win."

And with the victory Sunday, Baltimore advances to face the Broncos in next week's divisional round game. Denver beat the Ravens 34-17 in Baltimore Dec. 16.

"Really looking forward to it," Boldin said of the rematch with the Broncos. "I was hoping we'd get Denver." ■

Pro Bowl guard Marshal Yanda blocks Colts defensive tackle Ricardo Mathews, clearing space for quarterback Joe Flacco during the Ravens' 24-9 victory. DYLAN SLAGLE/STAFF PHOTO

This Time, Kick Is Good

Ravens come back, top No. 1 seed Broncos in classic

By Matt Zenitz

Trindon Holliday had two returns for touchdowns. Peyton Manning had three scoring passes. And the Baltimore Ravens found themselves trailing by a touchdown 70 yards from a tying score with no time-outs and less than a minute remaining.

This was a game that the Ravens weren't supposed to win.

But for every big play Denver made, and for every adverse situation Baltimore found itself in, the Ravens had an answer.

And behind a game-tying 70-yard touchdown pass from Joe Flacco with 31 seconds left in the fourth quarter, and a Corey Graham interception of Peyton Manning in overtime that set up a Justin Tucker game-winning field goal, Baltimore stunned the top-seeded Broncos with a 38-35 double overtime victory in Saturday's AFC divisional play-off game at Denver's Sports Authority Field at Mile High Stadium.

With the win, the Ravens advance to the AFC Championship Game for the second straight year. They'll travel to face the winner of today's divisional round game between the New England Patriots and the Houston Texans.

"It was a fight," Ravens running back Ray Rice said. "We didn't play perfect, but what you saw was a team that gave every ounce of energy they had out there — even with all of the undeniable factors against us. Just think about it: You give up two special teams touchdowns, and with the way Peyton played, odds say we're going to lose. But I think we're the only group of people ... that believed that we could get it done, and we did it."

But not without some late heroics from Flacco.

The Ravens trailed 35-28 with less than a minute left in the fourth quarter. They had no timeouts and were facing a third-and-3 at their own 30-yard line. But, just minutes after dropping a critical third-down pass on Baltimore's previous possession, Jacoby Jones got behind the

Wide receiver Jacoby Jones (12) celebrates with Torrey Smith (82) after his spectacular, game-tying 70-yard touchdown reception with 31 seconds left in regulation. AP Images

Broncos' defense along the right sideline and Flacco hit him stride for a stunning game-tying 70-yard score.

"It was crazy," Flacco said. "We called four [vertical routes], and I started to step up in the pocket and I kept my eye on the safeties depth at that point. I felt I had maybe a shot of getting it over them. At that point in the game, you don't have any timeouts and you have to go a pretty good length. You have to start taking shots at some point, and it happened to work out."

But after Denver's defense forced two Ravens punts to begin overtime, Baltimore's defense came up with a defining play of its own — with Graham diving in front of Broncos wide receiver Brandon Stokley to intercept Manning and set the Ravens' offense up at Denver's 45-yard line.

Ray Rice reeled off an 11-yard run just two plays later. And just four plays following Rice's run, Tucker drilled a 47-yard game-winning field goal to propel Baltimore to its second straight AFC championship game appearance.

"Thanks for bearing witness to one of the greatest football games you're ever going to see.... That football game did the game of football proud," Ravens head coach John Harbaugh said. "I'm so proud and grateful to have a chance to be associated with this game ... and grateful for the opportunity to stand with a bunch of men like that — through an incredible amount of adversity stood together, never wavered and never cracked."

Including Flacco.

Facing a defense that ranked third in the NFL against the pass during the regular season, Flacco threw for 331 yards and three touchdowns, including the dramatic game-tying 70-yard scoring pass to Jones late in the fourth quarter.

In his second game after returning from a torn triceps, linebacker Ray Lewis corrals Denver running back Ronnie Hillman. Lewis totaled 17 tackles on the day. AP Images

"Our offense goes through Joe," Rice said. "So when Joe plays at a high level like that, it makes everything a lot smoother. The way Joe was throwing the ball set up the running game in the second half. We were able to churn up yards in the running game because of the way Joe was [throwing the ball] and being on-point."

And just four weeks after being held scoreless on 10 of their first 11 possessions amid a 34-17 loss to this same Broncos team, Baltimore accumulated 479 yards and 21 first downs, keeping pace with a Denver team that got three touchdown passes from Manning and the two returns for scores from Holliday.

But it wasn't just Flacco.

Rice rushed for 131 yards and a touchdown and the Ravens' offensive line held the AFC's top-rated pass rush during the regular season to just one sack.

Baltimore rested most of its starters for its regular season finale, but it had a season-high 533 yards amid a 33-14 victory against the New York Giants a week earlier and 439 yards during its 24-9 wild-card victory over the Indianapolis Colts last week.

"We knew that we were rolling on offense a little bit," Ravens tight end Dennis Pitta said.

"We knew we weren't going to play like we did last time against them. We felt really good about this game, and we were able to execute, make a lot of big plays and come out with the win."

Said Rice: "The greatest part about this win is that we're going to celebrate. We're going to have the best plane ride back. I promise you, it's going to be a party on the plane. But as soon as we land, we're going to focus on the next team." ▪

Ravens wide receiver Torrey Smith, who repeatedly burned Pro Bowl Broncos cornerback Champ Bailey, catches one of his two touchdown passes against the Broncos. AP Images

AFC CHAMPIONSHIP GAME • JANUARY 20, 2013

Foxborough, Massachusetts • Ravens 28, Patriots 13

Redemption For Ravens

Flacco leads comeback as Ravens reach Super Bowl

By Matt Zenitz

This time, there was no crucial kick in the waning moments.

There was no last ditch effort at a game-tying score.

There was no need.

Joe Flacco threw three second-half touchdown passes. The defense held Tom Brady and the explosive New England Patriots offense scoreless after halftime. And for just the second time in franchise history, the Baltimore Ravens are going to the Super Bowl.

Almost a year to the day of a stunning defeat to the Patriots in last year's AFC title game, when Lee Evans dropped a would-be game-winning touchdown and Billy Cundiff missed a field goal to send it to overtime, the Ravens beat New England, 28-13, to advance Super Bowl XLVII.

Baltimore will face the San Francisco 49ers in New Orleans for the NFL championship on Feb. 3 in a game that will pit Baltimore coach John Harbaugh and his Ravens against his brother, Jim Harbaugh, and the 49ers.

"I have no words," Ravens safety Ed Reed said. "I'm just so grateful. I'm honestly just grateful."

It was just more than a month ago that Baltimore was in the midst of what Reed described as "the low point" of its season.

The team was in the midst of a three-game losing streak. The offense was sputtering. And the defense, decimated by injuries, was struggling as well. Six weeks later, the Ravens are AFC champions.

Baltimore trailed 13-7 at halftime, but Flacco threw three second half scoring passes and the Ravens' defense held the Patriots scoreless on each of their final six possessions.

Flacco actually started off slow Sunday. He completed just one of his first six pass attempts as Baltimore was forced to punt on each of its first three possessions.

From there, Flacco completed 20 of his next 28 pass attempts for 223 yards and three touchdowns.

He tossed a 5-yard scoring pass to

Joe Flacco's three second-half touchdown passes led the Ravens to a 28-13 win over the Patriots in the AFC Championship Game, avenging a loss to the Patriots a year earlier. AP Images

Dennis Pitta to give the Ravens a 14-13 lead midway through the third quarter. And after Baltimore's defense forced a New England punt, Flacco engineered another scoring drive, one he capped with a 3-yard touchdown pass to Anquan Boldin.

Flacco endured an uneven regular season, but he's thrown for a combined 853 yards and eight touchdowns without an interception in leading the Ravens to three playoff victories and a berth in the Super Bowl.

"We've always believed in Joe," Harbaugh said. "And for Joe to come out and have this kind of a game on this kind of a stage three weeks in a row … Joe's a great quarterback."

Added Baltimore tight end Ed Dickson: "Joe's continuing to play well in these playoffs, and the best is still yet to come. We've still got one more game."

Anquan Boldin, Torrey Smith and Dennis Pitta combined for 14 catches, 184 yards and three touchdowns. Boldin was held catchless in the first half, but he had five grabs for 60 yards and two scores in the second.

Boldin's second scoring catch, an 11-yarder, pushed Baltimore's lead to 28-13 with just more than 11 minutes left in the fourth quarter.

"We came into halftime and felt like we hadn't played our best ball," Boldin said. "But we wanted to just come out and play the way that we've been playing, and we wanted to up the tempo a little bit — just put the ball in the hands of our playmakers, and we were able to do that."

But the win was about more than the passing game.

The Patriots finished with 420 yards, but their final six possessions consisted of three turnovers, two punts and a turnover on downs.

Ravens safety Bernard Pollard had a crushing hit on New England running back Stevan Ridley early in the fourth quarter that led to a Ridley fumble that was recovered by Baltimore defensive end Arthur Jones.

Running back Ray Rice breaks the tackle of rookie Patriots linebacker Dont'a Hightower to score a second-quarter touchdown. AP Images

Flacco threw the 11-yard touchdown to Boldin just four plays later.

Harbaugh called Pollard's forced fumble "the turning point in the game."

"It was a team victory," Harbaugh said. "It was about the team. ... And to come out and play the way we did and win this football game means a lot."

And now, the journey continues — with just one game standing between the Ravens and the second Super Bowl championship in franchise history.

"We've definitely overcome a lot," Flacco said. "But I think when you look at the Super Bowl winners the past few years, I'd say they probably have a lot in common with that. It's about who can get ready and who can become their best at the right time."

Added Suggs: "We've still got one more to win and we're not satisfied." ■

Left: Part of a defensive effort that shut out New England in the second half, defensive lineman Haloti Ngata pressures Patriots quarterback Tom Brady. Above: Joe Flacco talks with Patriots quarterback Tom Brady, who he bested twice during the 2012-13 season, following the AFC Championship Game. AP Images